E. M. BOUNDS ON PRAYER

31 POWERFUL INSIGHTS TO STRENGTHEN YOUR PRAYER LIFE.

GODLIPRESS TEAM

© **Copyright 2022 by Godlipress. All rights reserved.**

This book is copyright protected. You cannot amend, distribute, sell, use, quote or paraphrase any part, or the content within this book, without the consent of the author or publisher, except in the case of brief quotations embodied in critical articles or reviews.

Scripture quotations are from The ESV® Bible (The Holy Bible, English Standard Version®), copyright © 2001 by Crossway, a publishing ministry of Good News Publishers. Used by permission. All rights reserved

CONTENTS

Introduction   vii

1. WHAT IS PRAYER?   1
   Daily Reflection   4

2. HOW OFTEN SHOULD WE PRAY?   5
   Daily Reflection   8

3. PRAYER WITH PROMISE   10
   Daily Reflection   13

4. OUR FATHER IN HEAVEN   14
   Daily Reflection   17

5. HOW TO PRAY IN THE HOLY SPIRIT   18
   Daily Reflection   21

6. WHEN IS THE BEST TIME TO PRAY?   22
   Daily Reflection   25

7. PRIVILEGE OR OBLIGATION?   26
   Daily Reflection   29

8. WHAT IS GOD'S WILL?   30
   Daily Reflection   33

9. HUMILITY IN PRAYER   34
   Daily Reflection   37

10. PRAYER IN TIMES OF TROUBLE   38
    Daily Reflection   41

11. COMPASSION IN PRAYER   42
    Daily Reflection   45

12. PRAYING FOR THE HARVEST   46
    Daily Reflection   49

13. SEEKING LIKE A CHILD	50
Daily Reflection	53
14. ASK OF ME	54
Daily Reflection	57
15. WHAT IS REVIVAL PRAYER?	58
Daily Reflection	61
16. ARE SHORT PRAYERS ENOUGH?	62
Daily Reflection	65
17. PRAYER IS AN INHERITANCE	66
Daily Reflection	69
18. PRAYING IS OF THE HEART	70
Daily Reflection	73
19. IS THERE SUCH A THING AS PRAYERLESS PRAYING?	74
Daily Reflection	77
20. PRAYING WITH FAITH	78
Daily Reflection	81
21. PRAYER AND SUPPLICATION	82
Daily Reflection	85
22. DO YOU TRUST GOD IN PRAYER?	87
Daily Reflection	90
23. PASSIONATE AND FERVENT PRAYER	91
Daily Reflection	94
24. OBEYING AND PRAYING	96
Daily Reflection	99
25. BY PRAYER AND THANKSGIVING	101
Daily Reflection	104
26. CAN PRAYER STILL BRING MIRACLES?	106
Daily Reflection	109
27. BE PERSISTENT IN PRAYER	110
Daily Reflection	113

28. PRAYER: THE CURE FOR ANXIETY?   115
    Daily Reflection   118

29. THE POWER OF INTERCESSORY PRAYER   119
    Daily Reflection   122

30. THE POWER OF A PRAYING PASTOR   123
    Daily Reflection   126

31. WHATEVER YOU ASK IN MY NAME   127
    Daily Reflection   130

About E. M. Bounds   131
References   133

INTRODUCTION

Some of the most incredible, hard-hitting, and revealing words on prayer came from the pen of E.M. Bounds. Of the 11 books he wrote, 9 of them are centered on this topic. For over a century, pastors, Christians, and teachers have been using his words for guidance and inspiration for their own communication with God. They have all become sought-after classics to this day.

Who better to draw from on the subject than a man who brought revival to his region through prayer meetings? Known as a person who spent hours every day with God, he not only wrote about prayer, he practiced it.

Bringing these truths to modern readers meant having a careful understanding of the text and meaning without losing anything along the way. Older phrases and words have been adapted while holding onto the treasure of Bounds' insight and wisdom.

More than that, we have searched through all of his 9 books on prayer to create an easy-to-use devotional highlighting some of his most enlightening commentaries on the different aspects of prayer. It was not easy to choose from such a vast storehouse of spiritual wealth—what to include and what to leave out. In some instances, we have taken excerpts and passages from the different books and aligned them together according to the same themes.

To assist with this, we have included *Daily Reflections* at the end of each reading to assist in your study and quiet time. Our heart in creating this month-long daily devotional was to challenge, encourage, and hopefully bring you into a deeper relationship with Jesus as you realize the importance of the tool of prayer that is available to every one of us.

As Bounds himself said:

> "Those who know God the best are the richest and most powerful in prayer."

1
WHAT IS PRAYER?

"You will make your prayer to him, and he will hear you"
Job 22:27

Prayer is a serious service due to God, an adoration, worship, an approach to God for our request, presenting our desire, the expression of our need for Him, who supplies all needs, and who satisfies all desires; who, as a Father, finds His greatest pleasure in meeting the needs and granting the desires of His children. Prayer is the child's request, not to the air nor the world, but the Father. Prayer is the outstretched arms of the child for the Father's help. Prayer is the child's cry calling to the Father's ear, the Father's heart, and to the Father's ability, which the Father hears, feels, and wants to relieve. Prayer is seeking God's greatest good, which will not come if we do not pray.

Everywhere we are told that it is more important and urgent that people pray than those who are skilled in the homiletic didactics of prayer. It is a thing of the heart, not of the schools. It is more feeling than words. Praying is the best school in which to learn to pray. Prayer is the best dictionary to define the art and nature of praying.

Prayer is not just a habit performed by custom and memory, something that must be done, with its value placed on how well and perfect its performance is. Prayer is not a duty to fulfill an obligation and to quiet the conscience. Prayer is not just a privilege, a sacred indulgence to be taken advantage of when we want with no serious loss if we forget or neglect it.

Prayer is a passionate and believing cry to God for some specific thing. God's rule is to answer by giving the specific thing asked for. It may come with other gifts and graces. Strength, serenity, sweetness, and faith may come as the bearers of the gifts. But even they come because God hears and answers prayer.

Prayer is not an invention of man, an imaginative relief. Prayer is no boring, dead performance, but is God's enabling act for man—living and life-giving, joy and joy-giving. Prayer is the contact of a living soul with God. In prayer, God bends to kiss us, bless us, and help us in everything that He has planned or we will need. Prayer fills our emptiness with God's fullness. It fills man's poverty with God's riches. It puts away our weakness with God's strength. It removes our smallness with God's greatness. Prayer is God's plan to supply our great and continuous need with God's great and continuous abundance.

Prayer has to do with the entire person. Prayer takes in a person in their whole being, mind, soul, and body. It takes a whole person to pray, and prayer affects the entire person in its results. As the whole nature of a person enters into prayer, so everything that belongs to them benefits from it. The whole person must be given to God in praying. The largest results from praying come to those who give themselves, all of themselves, all that belongs to themselves, to God. This is the secret of full consecration, and this is a condition for successful praying—the type that brings the largest fruits.

It is our business to pray, and it takes courageous people to do it. It is a godly business to pray, and it takes godly people to do it. And it is godly people who give themselves entirely over to prayer. Prayer is far-reaching in its influence and its effects. It is an intense, important business to deal with God and His plans and purposes, and it takes whole-hearted people to do it. No half-hearted, half-brained, half-spirited effort will do for this serious, important, heavenly business. The whole heart, the whole brain, the whole spirit, must be in prayer.

Praying is no small, insignificant task. While children should be taught to pray when they are young, praying is no child's task. Prayer demands our whole nature. Prayer engages all the powers of our moral and spiritual nature. This explains Jesus' praying as described in Hebrews 5:7:

"In the days of his flesh, Jesus offered up prayers and supplications, with loud cries and tears, to him who was able to save him from death, and he was heard because of his reverence."

As the entire person is active in true, sincere, effective praying, the entire person, soul, mind, and body, receive the benefits of prayer.

Daily Reflection

Understanding what prayer is—and also what it is not—is a good place to start. In this first reading, we find a number of striking and clear definitions of prayer. Bounds wants to make sure that we are not confused.

1. Take the time to draw up two lists. **Prayer Is** and **Prayer Is Not**. Go through the reading and allocate Bounds' definitions to the appropriate lists.
2. What is your own definition of prayer?
3. What do you understand by the assertion that "praying is the best school in which to learn to pray"?
4. Looking at Hebrews 5:7 as an example of prayer, how much of your own praying is like this? Why?

2
HOW OFTEN SHOULD WE PRAY?

"They ought always to pray and not lose heart"
Luke 18:1

Jesus said these words to emphasize to His followers the urgency and the importance of prayer, and to set them an example that they were far too slow to copy.

The *'always'* speaks for itself. Prayer is not a meaningless function or duty to be squeezed into the busy day, and we are not obeying our Lord's command when we are content with a few minutes on our knees in the morning rush or late at night when we are tired. God is always listening; His ear is attentive to the cry of His child, but we can never get to know Him if we use prayer like we use the phone—for a few words of rushed conversation. Intimacy requires development. We can never know God as it is our privilege to know Him by brief, disjointed requests for personal favors and nothing more.

That is not the way to communicate with our King. The goal of prayer is the ear of God, a goal that can only be reached by patience and continuous waiting on Him, pouring out our hearts to Him and allowing Him to speak to us. This is the only way we can expect to know Him, and as we come to know Him better, we will spend more time in His presence and find that it is a constant and growing joy.

Always does not mean that we neglect the ordinary duties of life. It means the heart is in intimate contact with God and never out of conscious touch with the Father; it is always going out to Him in loving communion, and as soon as the mind is finished with other tasks, it naturally returns to God like a bird to its nest. What a beautiful concept of prayer if we look at it in this light, if we see it as a constant fellowship, an unbroken audience with the King. Then prayer is not a duty we must perform, but rather a privilege to be enjoyed, a rare delight that is always revealing some new beauty.

When we open our eyes in the morning, our thoughts instantly go up to heaven. For many Christians, the morning hours are the most precious part of the day, because they provide the opportunity for the fellowship that sets the day's program. And what better introduction to the unending glory and wonder of a new day than to spend it alone with God? It is said that Mr. Moody, at a time when no other place was available, kept his morning quiet time in the coal shed, pouring out his heart to God and finding in his precious Bible a true "feast of fat things."

But we do not pray *'always'*—that is the trouble with so many of us. We need to pray much more than we do and much longer than we do.

In Romans 12:12, we have the words, *"Be constant in prayer."* This is the same word used for the prayer of the disciples that ushered in Pentecost with all the blessings of the Holy Spirit. In Colossians 4:2, Paul repeats the word, *"Continue steadfastly in prayer."* The word in its background and root means strong, the ability to stay and persevere steadfastly, to hold fast and firm, and to give constant attention.

In Acts 6:4, it is translated, *"Give ourselves continually to prayer"* (NKJV). There is in it constancy, courage, and perseverance. It means giving attention, and such deep concern to it, to make it evident and controlling.

This is the demand to *'continue.'* Prayer is to be incessant, without stopping, the spirit and the life always in the attitude of prayer. The knees may not always be bent, the mouth may not always be saying words of prayer, but the spirit is always in the act of prayer.

There should be no adjustment of life or spirit for devotion. The praying spirit should rule and adjust at all times and occasions. Our activities and work should be performed in the same spirit as our devotion. Touch the person of God who understands prayer in this way, at any point, at any time, and a full current of prayer is seen flowing from them.

Little prayer is the characteristic of a backslidden age and a backslidden church. Whenever there is little praying in the pulpit or the pew, spiritual bankruptcy is imminent and inevitable.

The cause of God is not restricted to a commercial age, a cultured age, an age of education, or an age of money. But it has one golden age, and that is the age of prayer. When its leaders are people of prayer, when prayer is the prevailing element of worship, like the incense giving continual fragrance to its service, then the cause of God will be triumphant.

Daily Reflection

This is a question that we so often ask, and yet, if we are very honest, probably already know the answer to. How often should we pray? How long should we pray for? More than anything, it shows our own state of heart in needing a cut-off or relief from something that should be a joy, a pleasure, and a feast. Maybe that's why there are so many reminders and commands to pray 'always' and 'continually.'

1. How often do *you* pray? Be honest. Write down the amount of time you spend each day, or each week, praying.
2. Do you find it hard to always be in an attitude of prayer, even when you are at work or home busy with other things? Why?

3. What do you understand by the phrase, "Intimacy requires development"? How can we develop intimacy?
4. What are the results of praying 'always' and praying 'little'?

3

PRAYER WITH PROMISE

> *"He has granted to us his precious and very great promises, so that through them you may become partakers of the divine nature… For this very reason, make every effort to supplement your faith with virtue"*
> 2 Peter 1:4-5

Without the promise, prayer is eccentric and useless. Without prayer, the promise is vague, voiceless, and impersonal. The promise makes prayer determined and irresistible. Peter said that God has given us *"precious and very great promises,"* and for this reason, we are to *"supplement your faith with virtue."* It is the addition that makes the promises current and beneficial to us. It is prayer that makes the promises important, precious, and practical. Paul did not hesitate to declare that God's grace that was so richly promised to us was made effective by prayer. *"You also must help us by prayer"* (2 Cor. 1:11).

The promises of God are *"precious and very great,"* words that clearly indicate their great value and capabilities, as grounds on which to base our expectations in praying. No matter how very great and precious they are, their realization, the possibility, and the condition of that realization are based on prayer. How glorious are these promises to Christians and the whole church! How bright and fruitful does the harvest and glory of the future shine on us through the promises of God! Yet these promises never brought hope to bear fruit in a prayerless heart. Even if these promises were increased a thousand times in number and preciousness, they still could not bring glory to a prayerless church. Prayer makes the promise rich, fruitful, and conscious reality.

Prayer is a spiritual energy, and illustrated in its expanded, mighty working, makes way for and brings into practical realization the promises of God.

God's promises cover all things that relate to life and godliness—to body and soul—which have to do with time and eternity. These promises bless the present and stretch out to the limitless and eternal future. Prayer holds these promises in check and fulfillment. Promises are God's golden fruit to be plucked by the hand of prayer. Promises are God's incorruptible seed, to be sown and plowed by prayer.

Prayer and promises are interdependent. The promise inspires and energizes prayer, but prayer locates the promise and gives it realization and location. The promise is like the wonderful rain falling in full showers, but prayer, like the pipes, which transmit, preserve, and direct the rain, localizes and precipitates these promises until they become local and personal, and bless, refresh, and fertilize. Prayer takes hold of the promise and conducts it to its end, removes the obstacles, and makes a highway for the promise to its glorious fulfillment.

Prayer is based on the purpose and promise of God. Prayer is submission to God. Prayer has no disloyalty against God's will. It might cry out against some bitterness or burden we face—*"if you are willing, remove this cup from me"*—but it is covered with the sweetest and quickest submission: *"Nevertheless, not my will, but yours, be done"* (Luke 22:42).

But prayer is conscious conformity to God's will, based on the direct promise of God's Word, and under the guidance of the Holy Spirit. Nothing is more certain than the Word of God being the solid foundation of prayer. We pray just as we believe in God's Word. Prayer is based directly and specifically on God's revealed promises in Jesus. It has no other ground on which to base its plea. Everything else is unstable. Not our feelings, not our merits, not our works, but God's promise is the basis of faith and the solid ground of prayer.

The opposite is also true. God's promises are dependent on prayer to make them a conscious realization. The promises are worked in us, taken hold of by us, and held in the arms of faith by prayer. Prayer gives the promises their efficiency, localizes and holds onto them, and uses them. Prayer puts the promises to practical use. Prayer puts the promises as a seed in the fertile soil.

Promises, like the rain, are general. Prayer embodies, precipitates, and locates them for personal use. Prayer goes by faith into the great fruit orchard of God's precious and very great promises, and with hand and heart picks the ripest and richest fruit. The promises may sparkle and dazzle like electricity but are powerless until these dynamic, life-giving currents are chained by prayer, and are turned into the mighty forces that move and bless.

Daily Reflection

We often don't relate promises and prayers together, especially with such a strong connection as we read about here. According to Bounds, one without the other is useless. It is imperative, then, to understand them both and to understand how they support and coexist in order to fully enjoy the benefits.

1. What is your understanding of the promises of God?
2. Why is prayer important to God's promises? What function does it hold?
3. Bounds interrupts talking about promises and prayer with the verse from Luke 22:42. Why does he do this? What does it show?
4. What do you understand by the words, "promises are worked in us"?

4

OUR FATHER IN HEAVEN

"Our Father in heaven, hallowed be your name"
Matthew 6:9

Prayer is confiding in, and asking of, God the Father.

We see this in the pattern that was given: *"Our Father in heaven"* (Matt 6:9). At the grave of Lazarus, Jesus lifted up His eyes and said, *"Father"* (John 11:41). In His priestly prayer, Jesus lifted up His eyes to Heaven, and said, *"Father"* (John 17:1).

Personal, familiar, and paternal was the way He prayed. Strong, effective, touching, and tearful was how he prayed. We can see this as we read the words of Paul: *"In the days of his flesh, Jesus offered up prayers and supplications, with loud cries and tears, to him who was able to save him from death, and he was heard because of his reverence"* (Hebrews 5:7).

The Jewish law and the prophets knew something of God as a Father. Although their understanding was occasional and imperfect, they still had glimpses of the great truth of God's Fatherhood and our sonship.

This lesson of "The Lord's Prayer," which came in response to the disciples' request to be taught how to pray, is a reminder of the prayer sections of the Sermon on the Mount. It is the same great lesson of praying to *"Our Father in heaven,"* and is one of insistent persistence. No prayer lesson would be complete without it. It belongs to the first and last lessons in prayer. God's Fatherhood gives shape, value, and confidence to all our praying.

Jesus lays the foundation of prayer deep and strong with this basic principle. The law of prayer, the right to pray, rests on sonship. *"Our Father"* brings us into the closest relationship to God. Prayer is the child's approach, the child's plea, the child's right. It is the law of prayer that looks up, that lifts the eye up to *"Our Father in Heaven."*

Our Father's house is our home in Heaven. Heavenly citizenship and heavenly homesickness are in prayer. Prayer is an appeal from the low, empty needs of earth, up to the high, full, all-sufficiency of Heaven. Prayer turns the eye and the heart up to Heaven with the longing, trust, and expectancy of a child. To lift up God's Name, to speak it with reverence, also belongs to prayer.

God as a King, with all of His authority, unites with His relation to us as a compassionate Father to secure the answer to prayer.

Jesus is fully committed to the answer of prayer. *"Whatever you ask in my name, this I will do, that the Father may be glorified in the Son"* (John 14:13). How assured the answer to prayer is when that answer is to glorify God the Father! And how eager Jesus is to glorify His Father in heaven! So eager that no prayer offered in His name is denied or overlooked by Him.

The answer to prayer is assured not only by the promises of God but by God's relation to us as a Father. *"But when you pray, go into your room and shut the door and pray to your Father who is in secret. And your Father who sees in secret will reward you"* (Matt. 6:6).

And again, we have these words as a confirmation of God as a Father acting on our behalf: *"If you then, who are evil, know how to give good gifts to your children, how much more will your Father who is in heaven give good things to those who ask him!"* (Matt. 7:11).

The only way to Heaven is by prayer of the heart. It is by prayer—not logic and reasoning that comes from studying. It is by prayer—not using our imagination or many wandering thoughts—it is the simple, confidential prayer of a child to their Father in Heaven.

Daily Reflection

The Lord's Prayer has become such an institution and a form of prayer to us that in many ways, it has lost its meaning and potency. But in today's reading, instead of trying to unpack the meaning of each line, Bounds simply directs us to *who* we are addressing! When we stop and realize this, everything that follows will change.

1. What do you understand by the term, 'Father God'?
2. Read 2 Corinthians 6:18 and Psalm 103:13. What is the impact of you being a *child* of God?
3. What is the significance of having God as a king and God as a Father?
4. In all His prayers, it is evident that Jesus wanted to bring glory to His Father. Is this true of the prayers you pray?

5

HOW TO PRAY IN THE HOLY SPIRIT

"Likewise the Spirit helps us in our weakness. For we do not know what to pray for as we ought, but the Spirit himself intercedes for us with groanings too deep for words"
Romans 8:26

The Holy Spirit helps us in our weaknesses, gives wisdom to our ignorance, turns ignorance into wisdom, and changes our weakness into strength. The Spirit Himself does this. He helps and takes hold with us as we tug and strive. He pleads for us and in us. He motivates and inspires our prayers. He works powerfully in us so that we can pray powerfully. He enables us to pray according to the will of God.

How can we know the will of God in our praying? What are the things that God designs especially for us to do and pray? The Holy Spirit reveals them to us.

"And he who searches hearts knows what is the mind of the Spirit, because the Spirit intercedes for the saints according to the will of God" (Rom. 8:27).

Combine this verse with Paul's words in 1 Cor. 2:10-12:

"These things God has revealed to us through the Spirit. For the Spirit searches everything, even the depths of God. For who knows a person's thoughts except the spirit of that person, which is in him? So also no one comprehends the thoughts of God except the Spirit of God. Now we have received not the spirit of the world, but the Spirit who is from God, that we might understand the things freely given us by God."

"Revealed to us through the Spirit." Note those words. The Spirit who lives in our hearts searches the deep purposes and the will of God to us, and reveals those purposes and that will of God, "that we might understand the things freely given us by God." Our spirits are so in tune with the Spirit, so responsive and obedient to His revelation and His will, that we ask with boldness and freedom the things which the Spirit has shown us as the will of God, and faith is assured.

The natural man prays but prays according to his own will, fancy, and desire. If he has passionate desires and groanings, they are the fire and agony of nature and not of the Spirit. How much natural praying takes place—selfish, self-contented, self-inspired? The Spirit, when He prays through us, focuses our praying on the will of God, and then we give our heart and expression to His unutterable groanings. Then we have the mind of Christ and pray as He would pray. His thoughts, purposes, and desires are our desires, purposes, and thoughts.

This is not a new and different Bible, but it is the Bible we have applied personally by the Spirit of God. It is not new verses, but rather the Spirit's embellishing of certain verses for us at the time.

It is the unfolding of the word by the Spirit's light, guidance, and teaching, enabling us to be intercessors on earth, in harmony with the great intercessions of Jesus at the Father's right hand in Heaven.

We have in the Holy Spirit an example and helper of what intercession is and should be. We are told to plead and pray in the Holy Spirit. We are reminded that the Holy Spirit *"helps us in our weakness,"* and that while intercession is a skill that is spiritual and we do not know what to pray for, yet the Spirit teaches us by making intercession in us *"groanings too deep for words"* (Rom. 8:26). How deep and heavy these intercessions of the Holy Spirit are! How profoundly He feels the world's sin, the world's sorrow, and the world's loss, and He sympathizes with the desperate conditions. This can be seen in His groanings which are too deep for words and too sacred to be voiced by Him. He inspires us to this godliest work of intercession, and His strength enables us to sigh to God for the oppressed, burdened, and distressed creation. The Holy Spirit helps us in many ways.

We always pray according to the will of God when the Holy Spirit helps our praying. He prays through us only *"according to the will of God."* If our prayers are not according to the will of God, they die in the presence of the Holy Spirit. He gives such prayers no attention, no help. Unnoticed and unhelped by Him, any prayers that are not according to God's will soon die out of every heart where the Holy Spirit lives.

Jude tells us we should be, *"praying in the Holy Spirit"* (Jude 1:20). As Paul says, *"praying at all times in the Spirit, with all prayer and supplication"* (Eph. 6:18). Never forgetting that: *"Likewise the Spirit helps us in our weakness. For we do not know what to pray for as we ought, but the Spirit himself intercedes for us with groanings too deep for words"* (Rom. 8:26).

Daily Reflection

Prayer is a spiritual exercise, a communion between our hearts and God. It is no surprise, then, that the Holy Spirit needs to be actively involved. But often, we don't know where our task ends and the Holy Spirit takes over. This reading brings some clarity to us, so our devotion will become effective and powerful in the Spirit.

1. What is the difference between the way the natural man prays and the spiritual man?
2. What weaknesses is the verse referring to?
3. How does the Holy Spirit help us understand the Bible better as we pray?
4. What is the important correlation between the will of God and the Holy Spirit when it comes to prayer?

6
WHEN IS THE BEST TIME TO PRAY?

"O Lord, in the morning you hear my voice; in the morning I prepare a sacrifice for you and watch"
Psalms 5:3

Those who have done the most for God in this world have been on their knees early in the morning. The people who waste the opportunity and freshness on other things rather than seeking God will struggle to seek Him during the rest of the day. If God is not first in our thoughts and efforts in the morning, He will be in the last place the remainder of the day.

Behind this early rising and early praying is the strong desire to pursue God. Morning laziness is the sign of a lifeless heart that has lost its enjoyment of God. David's heart was passionate for God. He hungered and thirsted after God, and so he met with God early, before daylight. Sleep could not chain his heart in its eagerness for God. Jesus longed for communion with God, so he woke before sunrise and went out into the mountain to pray. When the disciples awoke, ashamed at sleeping in, they would know where to find Him. We could go through the list of people who have made an impression on the world for God, and we would find them seeking early after God.

A desire for God that cannot break the chains of sleep is a weak thing and will do little good for God once it has indulged itself. A desire for God that stays so far behind the devil and the world at the beginning of the day will never catch up.

It is not simply getting up that puts those mighty people in the front to be able to command God's hosts, but it is the passionate desire which motivates and breaks all self-indulgent chains. Getting up gives release, increase, and strength to the desire. If those people had stayed in bed and indulged themselves, the desire would have been quenched. Acting on their desire for God allowed their faith to take hold of God and gave their hearts a wonderful revelation of Him. This strength of faith and fullness of revelation made them saints, and we can enjoy their accomplishments. But we are happy just to enjoy and not do it ourselves. We build their tombs and write their epitaphs, but we don't follow their examples.

More time and early mornings spent in prayer would revive and invigorate many spiritual lives that have backslidden. More time and early mornings in prayer would result in holy living. A holy life would not be so rare or so difficult if our devotions were not so short and rushed. A Christ-like attitude would not be so strange and hopeless if our quiet times were longer and more intense.

We live badly because we pray stingily. Plenty of time to feast in our quiet times will bring fulfillment and satisfaction to our lives. Our ability to stay with God in our prayer room measures our ability to stay with God out of the prayer room. Rushed quiet times are deceptive, defaulting. We are not only deceived by them, but we are losers because of them. Taking our time in personal devotions, we will be instructed and win the greatest victories. These are often the results of waiting—waiting until words and plans are exhausted, and silent and patient waiting gains the crown. Jesus asks with an offended emphasis, *"And will not God give justice to his elect, who cry to him day and night?"* (Luke 18:7).

We need a generation of pastors who seek God early, who give the freshness and dew of their efforts to God, and secure a fresh, fullness of His power that He may be like dew to them, full of joy and strength through the heat and work of the day.

Our laziness after God is our crying sin. The children of this world are wiser than we are. They are busy early and late. We do not seek God with passion and diligence. No one finds God if they do not follow hard after Him, and no heart follows hard after God if it is not seeking Him early in the morning.

Daily Reflection

This is another practical question that we often want to be answered: When is the best time to pray? Obviously, every person is different, our circumstances and abilities, but if we are looking for a guideline, then a very clear one has been drawn for us already. Biblically, in Jesus' life, and historically in many different men of God, it was often in the morning.

1. Why do you think early in the morning is the best time for prayer?
2. Why do you think most of us struggle to spend more time and early mornings praying?
3. Do you find it easy to pray early? Why?
4. Read Paul's words in 1 Corinthians 9:27. Do you think this relates to getting up and praying early?

7
PRIVILEGE OR OBLIGATION?

"Let us then with confidence draw near to the throne of grace, that we may receive mercy and find grace to help in time of need"
Hebrews 4:16

The Bible increases our faith in the belief that prayer affects God and secures blessings from God that we cannot get if we do not pray. The Bible illustrates the great truth that God hears and answers prayer. One of God's purposes in the Bible is to show us the importance, the priceless value, and the absolute necessity of asking God for the things we need now and for eternity. He urges us and warns us. He points us to Jesus, sent for our good, as His promise that prayer will be answered, teaching us that God is our Father, able to do all things and give all things to us, more than our earthly parents can do.

Let us understand ourselves and understand the matter of prayer. Our one duty is prayer, and we will never do it well unless we stick to it with everything we have. We will never do it well without finding the best ways to do it properly. Satan has suffered so much by good praying that all his cunning ways are used to try and cripple us from doing it well.

With everything we have, we must tie ourselves to prayer. To be loose and careless in it is to open the door to Satan. To be exact, prompt, unswerving, and careful in even the little things is to strengthen ourselves against the Evil One.

Prayer is a privilege—a sacred privilege. Prayer is a duty—a binding obligation, that we should be answerable for. But prayer is more than a privilege, more than a duty. It is a means, an instrument, a condition. Not praying is to lose out on much more than failing to do it or the enjoyment of a privilege. Not praying is to fail even more than not fulfilling an obligation.

Prayer is the appointed method of getting God's help. This help is as limitless as God's ability, and as varied and never-ending as our needs. Prayer is the channel through which good things flow from God to us, and all good flows from us to others. God is our Father—asking and giving are part of that relationship.

We are the ones more immediately concerned with praying. Our logic is dignified and is most spiritually engaged when used in prayer. Prayer makes our reason and rationality shine. The highest intelligence approves prayer—the wisest person is the one who prays the most and the best. Prayer is the school of wisdom as well as holiness.

The diary of Lady Maxwell of Edinburgh, who was very involved in funding schools under John Wesley's teaching, shows some rich advice for prayer and holy living.

One entry says:

Lately, I feel painfully convinced that I do not pray enough. Lord, give me the spirit of prayer and supplication. Oh, what a cause of thankfulness it is that we have a gracious God that we can go to on all occasions! Use and enjoy this privilege and you can never be miserable. Who gives thanks for this royal privilege? It puts God in everything, His wisdom, power, control, and safety. Oh, what an unspeakable privilege is prayer! Let us give thanks for it.

Prayer is not a picture to handle, admire, and look at. It is not beauty, coloring, shape, attitude, imagination, or genius. These things have nothing to do with its character or conduct. It is not poetry or music. Its inspiration and melody come from Heaven. Prayer belongs to the spirit, and sometimes possesses our spirit and motivates it with a high and holy purpose.

When we look at the Bible, we see that there is no duty more demanding and necessary than that of prayer. On the other hand, we discover that no privilege is more exalted, no habit more richly owned by God. There are no promises more radiant, more abundant, more explicit, more repeated, than those that are attached to prayer.

Daily Reflection

For many of us, being a Christian comes with certain tasks that we simply have to fulfill in order to be good or successful at it. We have to pray, read the Bible, go to church, and do other duties that we often feel obliged to do. But in this reading, we find that prayer is not just a task to be completed because we have to, but also a privilege!

1. Do you find prayer to be more of a privilege or an obligation in your life?
2. Why do you think Satan focuses much of his attention on 'crippling' prayer?
3. Bounds admits that it is a privilege and an obligation, but then he says that it 'is more' than both of these. What does he mean?
4. Do you agree with the statement, "There is no duty more demanding and necessary than that of prayer"?

8

WHAT IS GOD'S WILL?

"And this is the confidence that we have toward him, that if we ask anything according to his will he hears us"
1 John 5:14

What is God's will about prayer? First, it is God's will that we pray.

Jesus Christ *"told them a parable to the effect that they ought always to pray and not lose heart"* (Luke 18:1). Paul writes to Timothy about the things that Christians should do, and the first aspect he lists before all the others is prayer: *"First of all, then, I urge that supplications, prayers, intercessions, and thanksgivings be made for all people"* (1 Tim. 2:1).

In connection with these words, Paul declares that the will of God and the redemption and mediation of Jesus for the salvation of all men are all vitally linked in prayer. His apostolical authority and concern for people's hearts line up with God's will and Jesus' intercession *"that in every place the men should pray"* (1 Tim. 2:8).

Notice how often prayer is mentioned in the New Testament:

- *"Be constant in prayer"* (Rom. 12:12)
- *"Pray without ceasing"* (1 Thess. 5:17)
- *"Continue steadfastly in prayer, being watchful in it with thanksgiving"* (Col. 4:2)
- *"Be self-controlled and sober-minded for the sake of your prayers"* (1 Peter 4:7)
- Jesus' clear command was *"Watch and pray"* (Matt. 26:41).

What are all these and others, if not the will of God that men should pray?

Prayer is complementary, cooperates with, and makes God's will effective—His sovereign plan is to run parallel to the atonement of Jesus in all its power. It was through the Holy Spirit and by the grace of God that He would "taste death for everyone." It is through the Holy Spirit and by the grace of God that we can pray for every man.

But how do I know that I am praying by the will of God?

Every true attempt to pray is in response to the will of God. You might not do it correctly and might not be taught well by human teachers, but it is acceptable to God because it is in obedience to His will. If I give myself up to the inspiration of the Spirit of God, who commands me to pray, the details and the requests of that prayer will all come into harmony with the will of Him who wills that I should pray.

Prayer is not a little thing; it is not a selfish or small matter. It does not concern the trivial interests of one person. The smallest prayer is expanded by the will of God until it touches every word, confirms every interest, enhances our riches in Him, and reveals God's goodness.

Jesus' life was in the image of His Father. He was the *"exact imprint of his nature"* (Heb. 1:3). And so the spirit of prayer with Jesus was to do God's will. He constantly claimed that He came to do His Father's will and not His own. When the crisis came in His life in Gethsemane and all its darkness, with the crushing weight of man's sins and sorrows pressing down on Him, His spirit crushed—almost dying—He cried out for relief, yet it was not His will that was to be followed. It was only an appeal out of weakness and death for God's relief in God's way. God's will was to be the law and the rule of His relief if relief came.

So those who follow Christ in prayer must have God's will as their law, rule, and inspiration.

Jesus prayed always with this one exception in conformity with the will of God. He was one with God's plan, and one with God's will. To pray in conformity with God's will was the life and law of Christ. The same was the law of His praying.

Conformity means to *"stand mature and fully assured in all the will of God"* (Col. 4:12). It means to delight in doing God's will, to run passionately to carry out His plans. Conformity to God's will involves submission—patient, loving, sweet submission. But submission by itself falls short of and does not include conformity. We may be submissive but not conformed. We may accept results against which we have struggled, and even be resigned to them.

Conformity means to be one with God, both in the result and in processes. Submission may be one with God in the end. Conformity is one with God at the beginning and the end. Jesus had conformity, absolute and perfect, to God's will, and that was how He prayed.

Daily Reflection

One of the timeless questions that are asked by every Christian is: What is God's will for this situation, for my life? Here, Bounds takes it a step further and looks at God's will in our prayers. Are we praying correctly? Do we pray in line with God's plans? Do we know what God wants so that we can pray accordingly? The answer can be found in the way Jesus prayed.

1. God's will is that we pray. Do you agree with this statement? Why?
2. "Every true attempt to pray is in response to the will of God." What do you understand by this?
3. Bounds uses the word 'conformity.' Why is this necessary in praying according to God's will? Do you find it easy or not?
4. How can we conform more to God's will?

9
HUMILITY IN PRAYER

"If my people who are called by my name humble themselves, and pray and seek my face and turn from their wicked ways, then I will hear from heaven and will forgive their sin and heal their land"
2 Chronicles 7:14

Humility is an indispensable part of true prayer. It must be an attribute, a characteristic of prayer. Humility must be in the character of praying as light is of the sun. Prayer has no beginning, no end, and no being, without humility. As a ship is made for the sea, so prayer is made for humility, and so humility is made for prayer.

Humility is not an abstraction from self, nor does it ignore thoughts about self. It is a principle with many parts. Humility is born by looking at God and His holiness and then looking at self and man's unholiness. Humility loves obscurity and silence, hates applause, lifts others up before itself, excuses their faults, forgives easily, is less worried about being mocked, and sees pride as useless and false.

True honor and greatness are in humility. It knows and reveres the riches of the cross, and the humiliations of Jesus. It fears the shine of those characteristics that people admire and loves those that are more secret and which are prized by God. It finds comfort in its own weakness. It prefers contrition before the fame of the world.

We see the grace of humility in the tax collector's prayer, but not in that of the Pharisee.

Humility holds the life of prayer. Pride and vanity cannot pray. But, humility is more than the absence of vanity and pride. It is a positive quality, a force that energizes prayer. It comes from a low estimation of ourselves and what we deserve. The Pharisee did not pray, even though he was taught and expected to pray, because there was no humility in his praying. The tax collector prayed, even though he was rejected by the public because he prayed in humility.

To be clothed with humility is to be clothed with an outfit of prayer. Humility is feeling little because we are little. Humility is realizing our unworthiness because we are unworthy, feeling and declaring ourselves as sinners because we are sinners. Kneeling becomes our attitude of prayer because it shows humility.

The Pharisee's proud estimate of himself and his disgust for his neighbor closed the gates of prayer to him.

On that day many will say to me, "Lord, Lord, did we not prophesy in your name, and cast out demons in your name, and do many mighty works in your name?' And then will I declare to them, 'I never knew you; depart from me, you workers of lawlessness." (Matt. 7:22-23)

Humility is the first and last attribute of Christianity and the first and last attribute of praying. There is no Christ without humility. There is no praying without humility. If you want to learn the art of praying, then learn the lesson of humility.

How graceful and essential the attitude of humility becomes to us! Humility is one of the unchanging and challenging attitudes of prayer. Dust, ashes, earth on the head, sackcloth for the body, and fasting were the symbols of humility in the Old Testament. Sackcloth, fasting, and ashes brought Daniel into humility before God, and brought the angel Gabriel to him. The angels are fond of 'sackcloth-and-ashes' people.

How humble the attitude of Abraham, the friend of God, when begging for God not to destroy Sodom! *"I who am but dust and ashes"* (Gen. 18:27). With humility, Solomon appeared before God! His grandeur is brought low, and his glory and majesty are put aside as he assumes the correct attitude before God: *"I am but a little child. I do not know how to go out or come in"* (1 Kings 3:7).

The pride of doing sends its poison through all our praying. The same pride of being infects all our prayers, no matter how well-worded they may be. It was this lack of humility, this self-applauding, this self-exaltation, which kept the most religious man of Jesus' day from being accepted by God. And the same thing will keep us from being accepted by Him.

"O that now I might decrease!
O that all I am might cease!
Let me into nothing fall!
Let my Lord be all in all."

Daily Reflection

Humility is often a stumbling block in our spiritual lives because of our human nature that constantly tries to protect itself and elevate itself, rather than submit and surrender. Understanding the need for humility is a key aspect of approaching God so that our prayers are acceptable.

1. Looking at what Bounds says humility is and is not, what is your definition?
2. If you had to be very honest, are your prayers more like that of the Pharisee or the tax collector?
3. Do you sometimes fall into the trap of the "pride of doing" and the "pride of being"?
4. Read 1 Peter 5:5-6 and James 4:6-7. Comment on this, especially in terms of the way we need to pray.

10

PRAYER IN TIMES OF TROUBLE

"Rejoice in hope, be patient in tribulation, be constant in prayer"
Romans 12:12

Trouble and prayer are closely related to each other. Prayer is of great value to trouble. Trouble often drives us to God in prayer, while prayer is our voice in trouble. There is great value in prayer in the time of trouble. Prayer often delivers out of trouble, and more often gives strength to endure trouble, gives comfort in trouble, and brings patience in the midst of trouble. We are wise when, in times of trouble, we know our true source of strength and continue to pray.

Trouble belongs to the present state of people on earth. *"Man who is born of a woman is few of days and full of trouble"* (Job

14:1). Trouble is common to every person. There is no exception in any age, region, or status. Rich and poor, the educated and the ignorant, we are all part of this sad and painful inheritance of the fall of man. *"No temptation has overtaken you that is not common to man"* (1 Cor. 10:13). The day of trouble comes to everyone at some time in his life. *"The evil days come and the years draw near"* (Ecc. 12:1) when the heart feels its heavy pressure.

Prayer in our time of trouble brings comfort, help, hope, and blessings. Although it does not remove the hardship, it enables us to be able to bear it and submit to the will of God. Prayer opens our eyes to see God's hand in trouble. Prayer does not interpret God's provision and intervention, but it does justify them and recognize God in them. Prayer lets us see a good outcome in trouble. Prayer in trouble drives us away from unbelief, saves us from doubt, and keeps us from uselessly questioning everything because of our painful experiences.

Let us see the honor given to Job after surviving all his troubles: *"In all this Job did not sin or charge God with wrong"* (Job 1:22).

Unfortunately, ignorant, selfish people without faith in God and who do not know about the way God disciplines us blame Him when troubles come and are tempted to *"curse God"* (Job 2:9). How silly and selfish are the complaints, grumblings, and rebellion of people in times of trouble! We need to read the story of the Israelites in the desert again and see how useless all our worrying over trouble is, as if it could change things! *"And which of you by being anxious can add a single hour to his span of life?"* (Matt. 6:27). How much wiser, better, and easier it is to bear life's troubles when we take everything to God in prayer?

Trouble has good outcomes for those who pray, and they experience it that way. Like the Psalmist, we will be happy if we find that our troubles have been blessings in disguise. *"It is good for me that I was afflicted, that I might learn your statutes… I know, O Lord, that your rules are righteous, and that in faithfulness you have afflicted me"* (Psalm 119:71, 75).

Prayer in hardship brings our spirit into perfect submission to God's will, and our will is conformed to His will. It keeps us from grumbling about our circumstances and delivers us from having a rebellious heart or being critical of the Lord. Prayer sanctifies trouble to our benefit. Prayer prepares the heart and softens it under God's disciplining hand. Prayer puts us where God can bring to us spiritual and eternal blessings. Prayer allows God to work freely with us and in us in our hardships. Prayer allows God's servant, trouble, to accomplish its mission in us, with us, and for us. The end of trouble is always good in God's mind.

If trouble fails in its mission, it is either because of a lack of prayer or unbelief. Being in harmony with God always makes trouble a blessing. The good or evil of trouble is always determined by the spirit in which it is received. Trouble proves a blessing or a curse, according to how it is received and treated by us. It either softens or hardens us. It either draws us to prayer and God or it drives us further away.

Unfortunately, trouble does not always drive people to God in prayer. It is a sad case for those who, when trouble bends their spirit down and grieves their heart, yet do not know where the trouble comes from nor how to pray about it. Blessed is the person who is driven by trouble to his knees in prayer!

Daily Reflection

Most prayers happen when we are in trouble. We cry out for help or defense from some injustice. But we can see here that trouble is not just something to ask God to get us out of, but is often something that God puts us in to compel us to pray more and to seek Him.

1. When you are in times of trouble, is prayer your first and immediate response?
2. If prayer does "not remove the hardship," what does it do?
3. Do you share the same view as in Psalm 119:71: *"It is good for me that I was afflicted"*? Why?
4. What do you understand of the relationship between God's discipline and times of trouble?

11

COMPASSION IN PRAYER

"Finally, all of you be of one mind, having compassion for one another; love as brothers, be tenderhearted, be courteous"
1 Peter 3:8 NKJV

Spiritual compassion is born in a renewed heart and finds hospitality there. This compassion has the quality of mercy, and the nature of pity, and moves the soul with tenderness for others. Compassion is moved at the sight of sin, sorrow, and suffering. It is opposite to ignoring others' needs and is far from being hardened toward people in trouble. Compassion has sympathy for others, is interested in them, and is concerned about them.

Natural compassion uses its force in simple gifts to those in need. But spiritual compassion, in a renewed heart, is Christ-like and is deeper, wider, and more prayerlike. Christ-like compassion always moves to prayer. It goes beyond the relief of physical needs, and saying, *"Be warmed and filled"* (James 2:16). It reaches deeper down and goes much further.

Compassion is not blind. Someone who does not see the sinfulness of sin, the needs, and the sorrows of humanity will never have compassion for them. Jesus, *"when he saw the crowds, he had compassion for them"* (Matt. 9:36). First, seeing the people, with their hunger, their suffering, and their helpless condition, then compassion, then prayer for the multitudes. The person who sees and is unmoved by their sad state, unhappiness, and destruction is hard and not Christ-like. They have no heart of prayer for people.

Compassion may not always move us but is always moved toward us. Compassion may not always turn us to God, but it will turn God to us. And where it is helpless to relieve the needs of others, it can at least break out into prayer to God for others. Compassion is never indifferent, selfish, and forgetful of others.

But compassion is not just about physical disabilities and needs. The heart's terrible state, its needs, and danger all appeal to compassion. The highest state of grace is compassion for sinners. When compassion sees dying people rushing to the judgment of God, then it breaks out into intercession for sinful people.

Jeremiah declares this about God, giving the reason why sinners are not consumed by His anger and judgment: *"Through the Lord's mercies we are not consumed, because His compassions fail not"* (Lam. 3:22 NKJV).

And it is this godly quality in us that makes us so much like God. So we find the Psalmist describing the righteous man who is blessed by God: *"He is gracious, and full of compassion, and righteous"* (Psalm 112:4 NKJV).

And as though he was giving encouragement to repentant sinners, the Psalmist records some of the striking attributes of God's character: *"The Lord is gracious and full of compassion, slow to anger and great in mercy"* (Psalm 145:8 NKJV).

It is no wonder, then, that we find several records of Jesus, when He was on earth, *"had compassion for them"* (Matt. 9:36). Can anyone doubt that His compassion moved Him to pray for those suffering, hurting people who came across His pathway?

Paul was very interested in the spiritual welfare of the Jews, was concerned about them, and his heart was filled with tender compassion for their salvation, even though he was mistreated and severely persecuted by them. In writing to the Romans, he expresses himself:

I have great sorrow and unceasing anguish in my heart. For I could wish that I myself were accursed and cut off from Christ for the sake of my brothers, my kinsmen according to the flesh. (Rom. 9:1-4)

What a comfort and hope there is to fill our hearts when we think of one in Heaven who lives forever to intercede for us, because *"The steadfast love of the Lord never ceases"* (Lam. 3:22). Above everything else, we have a compassionate Savior, one *"He can deal gently with the ignorant and wayward, since he himself is beset with weakness"* (Heb. 5:2). The compassion of Jesus suits Him as the Great High Priest of Adam's fallen, lost, and helpless race.

And if He is filled with such compassion that it moves Him at the Father's right hand to intercede for us, then we should have the same compassion for the ignorant and those out of the way, under God's wrath, as would move us to pray for them.

As far as we are compassionate for others, we will be prayerful for others. Compassion does not waste its power by simply saying, *"be warmed and filled,"* but drives us to our knees in prayer for those who need Jesus and His grace.

Daily Reflection

Praying for others is expected of us—lifting people up in prayer. But in this reading, we find that it goes much deeper than simply listing people's needs and concerns. The term used here is compassion, which requires a much more intense response than sympathy.

1. What is the difference between natural and Christ-like compassion?
2. What do you understand by the words, "It will turn God to us"?
3. If compassion is not just about physical needs, then what is it about?
4. Are your prayers filled with natural sympathy or Jesus' love for others?

12

PRAYING FOR THE HARVEST

> *"Then he said to his disciples, 'The harvest is plentiful, but the laborers are few; therefore pray earnestly to the Lord of the harvest to send out laborers into his harvest'"*
> Matthew 9:37-38

The harvests need laborers. He did not call these laborers immediately, by sovereign authority, but charged the disciples to go to God in prayer and ask Him to send laborers into His harvest.

Here is the urgency of prayer enforced by the compassions of Jesus—born of compassion for perishing humanity. The church is urged to pray for laborers to be sent into the harvest of the Lord. The harvest will go to waste and perish without the workers—these workers must be God-chosen,

God-sent, and God-commissioned. But God does not send them into His harvest without prayer. The failure of the laborers is because of the failure of prayer. The scarcity of laborers in the harvest is due to the fact that the church fails to pray for them.

The gathering of the harvests of the earth for the storehouse of heaven is dependent on the prayers of God's people. Prayer makes sure the workers are sufficient in quantity and quality for all the needs of the harvest. God's chosen laborers are the only ones who will truly go, filled with Christ-like compassion and filled with His power—secured by prayer. Christians on their knees with Jesus' compassion in their hearts for dying people heading to eternal danger is the guarantee of laborers to meet the needs of the earth and the purposes of heaven.

God is sovereign, and the choice of laborers in His harvest He delegates to no one else. Prayer honors Him as sovereign and moves Him to His wise and holy selection. We will have to put prayer to the front before the fields of the lost will be successfully plowed for Jesus. God knows His people, and He knows His work. Prayer gets God to send the best, most suitable, and qualified to work in the harvest.

Fulfilling the missionary cause by methods without God has been its weakness and its failure. Compassion for the world of sinners, fallen in Adam but redeemed in Christ, will move the church to pray for them and to pray that the Lord of the harvest will send laborers out.

God's plan to find missionaries is the same plan He has for obtaining preachers—through praying. It is the prayer plan, different from all man-made plans. These mission workers are to be sent—God must send them. They are called by God, inwardly moved to enter the harvest fields of the world. People do not choose to be missionaries any more than they choose to be preachers. God sends out workers in His harvest field in answer to the prayers of His church.

And *he said to them, "The harvest is plentiful, but the laborers are few. Therefore pray earnestly to the Lord of the harvest to send out laborers into his harvest."* (Luke 10:2)

It is the business of the church to do the praying. It is God's business to call and send out the workers. God does not do the praying. The church does not do the calling. And just as Jesus was moved at the sight of weary, hungry, and scattered multitudes, so whenever the church sees the people on earth weary in soul, living in darkness, and wicked and sinful, it will be moved to compassion and begin to pray for the Lord of the harvest to send workers into His harvest.

Is the harvest great? Are the workers few? Then *"pray earnestly to the Lord of the harvest to send out laborers into his harvest."* Oh, that a great wave of prayer would sweep over the church asking God to send out an army of workers into the harvest fields of the earth! He who calls will provide the means for supporting those whom He calls and sends out.

The one great need in the modern missionary movement is intercessors. They were scarce in the days of Isaiah. This was his complaint:

"He saw that there was no man, and wondered that there was no one to intercede" (Isaiah 59:16).

So, today there is a great need for intercessors: first, for the needy harvest-fields of earth, born out of Christ-like compassion for the thousands without the Gospel; and then intercessors for workers to be sent out by God into the ripe fields of the earth.

Daily Reflection

Praying for others to be born again is very important, as it is in line with the Great Commission that Jesus gave us before returning to heaven. Praying for people to be sent out as missionaries or workers in the harvest is just as crucial. To pray for both is to fulfill the requirements of praying for sinners.

1. Why do you think the church always falls into the trap of doing missionary work "by methods without God"?
2. Do you have certain people that are not born again that you pray for?
3. Have you ever prayed that God will send someone to tell them about Jesus?
4. According to Bounds, what is the greatest need in missionary movements? Why?

13

SEEKING LIKE A CHILD

"Truly, I say to you, unless you turn and become like children, you will never enter the kingdom of heaven"
Matthew 18:3

The simplicity of prayer and its child-like elements form a great obstacle to true praying. Intellect gets in the way of the heart. Only the child-like spirit is the spirit of prayer. It is not an easy task to make an adult a child again. In song, poetry, and memory, they might wish they were a child again, but in prayer, they must be a child again in reality. At their mother's knee—simple, intense, direct, trustful—no doubt or temper to be denied. A desire that burns and consumes which can only be voiced by a cry. It is not easy to have this child-like spirit of prayer.

The person who truly prays gets many things from God that are denied to those who do not pray. The aim of all real praying is to get the thing that is prayed for, as the child's cry for bread is to get the bread. This view removes prayer from any religious performances. Prayer is not acting out a part or going through religious motions. Prayer is not official, formal, or ceremonial but direct, passionate, and intense. Prayer is not religious work that must be completed and succeeds because it was done well. Prayer is the helpless and needy child crying to the compassion of the Father's heart and the abundance and power of a Father's hand. The answer will come because the Father's heart can be touched and the Father's hand can be moved.

The object of asking is to receive. The aim of seeking is to find. The purpose of knocking is to call attention and get in. This is Jesus' repeated statement that the prayer without doubt will be answered—not in some roundabout way, but by getting the thing that was asked for.

The value of prayer does not lie in the number of prayers or the length of prayers, but its value is found in the truth that we are privileged in our relationship with God to bring Him our desires and make our requests known to Him; and He will grant them. The child asks because the parent is in the habit of granting the child's requests. As the children of God, when we need something and we need it badly, we go to God for it.

Prayer is not only based on a promise but on a relationship. The repentant sinner prays on a promise. The child of God prays on the relation of a child. What the father has belongs to the child for present and prospective uses. The child asks, and the father gives. The relationship is one of asking and answering, of giving and receiving. The child is dependent upon the father, must look to the father, must ask of the father, and must receive from the father.

We know how with earthly parents, asking and giving belong to this relation, and how in the act of asking and giving, the relationship of parent and child is cemented and enriched. The parent finds his pleasure and satisfaction in giving to an obedient child, and the child finds his pleasure in the father's loving and continuous giving.

Neither the Bible nor the child of God knows anything about that false belief that we must answer our own prayers. God answers prayer. The true Christian does not pray to motivate themselves, but their prayer is motivating themselves to take hold of God. The heart of faith does not know the skepticism that restricts prayer or dampens its passion by whispering that prayer does not affect God.

D. L. Moody told a story of a little girl whose parents had died, and who was taken into another family. The first night, she asked whether she could pray as she used to do. They said: "Oh, yes!" So she knelt down and prayed as her mother had taught her; and when that ended, she added a little prayer of her own: "God, make these people as kind to me as father and mother were." Then she paused and looked up, as if expecting the answer, and then added: "Of course, you will." How simple that little child's faith was! She expected God to answer and 'do,' and 'of course' she got her request, and that is the spirit in which God invites us to approach Him.

Daily Reflection

We know that we are called to have child-like faith in God, but it is not easy, especially when we are faced with trying to be adults dealing with adult problems. We get caught up in obligations, duties, and expectations, and we forget that God is our Father, and we are His children.

1. What is the "aim of all real praying"? How does this understanding change the concept of prayer?
2. Where is the value of prayer found?
3. Have you ever believed or found yourself believing that you have to try and answer your own prayers? Why is this wrong?
4. How can we become more like children in the way we pray?

14

ASK OF ME

"Ask of me, and I will make the nations your heritage, and the ends of the earth your possession"
-Psalm 2:8

"Whether we like it or not," said Charles Spurgeon, "asking is the rule of the kingdom. 'Ask, and it will be given to you' (Matt. 7:7). It is a rule that will never be changed in anybody's case. Jesus is like the elder brother of the family, but God has not relaxed the rule for Him. Remember Psalm 2:8. If the Son of God cannot be excused from the rule of asking that He may have, then you and I cannot expect the rule to be relaxed in our favor. Why should it be? What reason can there be that we should be excused from prayer? What argument can be made to deprive us of the privilege and deliver us from the necessity of supplication? I can see none: can you?"

"Ask of me." Ask of God. We have not depended on prayer. We have neglected the main condition of prayer. We have not prayed correctly. We have not prayed at all. God is willing to give, but we are slow to ask. The Son, through Christians, is always praying and God the Father is always answering.

"Ask of me." In the invitation, we find the assurance of the answer—the shout of victory is there if we have ears to hear it. The Father holds the authority and power in His hands. How easy is the condition, and yet we take so long to fulfill it! Nations are in bondage; there are countries that are still not possessed by the Gospel. The earth groans; the world is kept captive—Satan and evil have their way.

The Father is the Giver. *"Ask of me"* is the request that empowers and inspires all movements of the Father. The Gospel is inspired by God, and all its inspirations are found in prayer. *"Ask of me"* is behind every movement. Standing as the foundation of Jesus on the throne is the covenant of the Father, *"Ask of me, and I will make the nations your heritage, and the ends of the earth your possession"* (Psalm 2:8).

We can do all things with God's help and can have all of His help when we ask. The Gospel, in its success and power, depends on our ability to pray. The provision of God depends on man's ability to pray. We can have all that God has. *"Ask of me."* This is no figment of the imagination, no idle dream, no selfish desire. The life of the church is the highest life, and its function is to pray. Its prayer life is the highest life—fragrant and evident.

But not all praying is praying. The driving power, the conquering force in God's cause, is God Himself. *"Call to me and I will answer you, and will tell you great and hidden things that you have not known"* (Jer. 33:3) is God's challenge to prayer. Prayer puts God in full force into His work: *"Ask me of things to come; will you command me concerning my children and the work of my hands?"* (Isaiah 45:11). God's carte blanche to prayer.

Faith is only powerful when it is on its knees and its hands reach out and take hold of God, then it draws on God's full capacity; for only a praying faith can get God's promise to give you whatever you ask for. The Canaanite woman, the persistent widow, and the friend at midnight are lessons of what determined prayer can do in challenging conditions, changing defeat into victory and overcoming despair. Being one with Jesus, the height of spiritual attainment, is glorious in all things—mostly because we can then ask and it will be given. Prayer in Jesus' name puts the crowning glory on God because it glorifies Him through the Son and promises that the Son will give us whatever we ask for.

God shapes the life and success of His plans on prayer. It is a condition that He put there: *"Ask of me"* is the one condition that advances and brings victory to His plans.

"Ask of me" is the condition—a praying people who are willing and obedient. *"May prayer be made for him continually"* (Psalm 72:15). Under this simple promise, men and women in the Old Testament came before God. They prayed and God answered their prayers, and the cause of God was kept alive in the world by the flame of their praying. In the words of Charles Spurgeon:

God will bless Elijah and send rain on Israel, but Elijah must pray for it. If the chosen nation is to prosper, Samuel must beg for it. If the Jews are to be delivered, Daniel must intercede. God will bless Paul, and the nations shall be converted through him, but Paul must pray. He did pray without ceasing; his letters show that he expected nothing except by asking for it. To have everything by asking, and nothing without asking, I ask you to see how absolutely vital prayer is, and I beg you to grow in it.

Daily Reflection

Asking is the basis of most prayer. There is communication where we speak with God, tell Him how we feel, and let Him know our thoughts and worries, but at the end of it, prayer is to ask God for what we need and want. It is not a bad thing, it is expected of us. That is why Jesus told His disciples to do it—to ask Him. By taking hold of this aspect of prayer in its entirety, we can begin to pray with expectation.

1. What do you understand by the words, "Asking is the rule of the kingdom"?
2. Bounds says that asking is a 'condition.' What does he mean by this?
3. Why do you think God puts this emphasis on asking?
4. What is meant by, "Faith is only powerful when it is on its knees"?

15

WHAT IS REVIVAL PRAYER?

"I urge that supplications, prayers, intercessions, and thanksgivings be made for all people... it is pleasing in the sight of God our Savior, who desires all people to be saved and to come to the knowledge of the truth"
1 Timothy 2:1-4

All the true revivals have been born in prayer. When God's people become so concerned about the state of Christianity that they lie on their faces day and night in sincere prayer, the blessing will not fail.

It is the same all through history. Every revival recorded has been bathed in prayer. For example, the wonderful revival in Shotts (Scotland) in 1630. Several of the persecuted ministers would gather, and many others spent several days in prayer before the service. In the evening, instead of resting, the crowd divided themselves into groups and spent the whole night in supplication and praise. After a day of thanksgiving and praise, a young man called John Livingston was asked to preach. He had spent the night in prayer—but as the time drew near, he got scared and he left. But before he got far, he was reminded of those words "Was I ever a barren wilderness or a land of darkness?" and returned. He preached from Ezekiel 36:25-26 for two hours. Five hundred conversions followed that one sermon.

Richard Baxter was said to have "stained his study walls with a praying breath, and after becoming anointed with the anointing of the Holy Spirit he sent a river of living water over Kidderminster." Whitfield once prayed, "O Lord, give me souls or take my soul." After much pleading, "he once went to the Devil's fair and took more than a thousand souls out of the paw of the lion in a single day."

Mr. Finney says:

I once knew a minister who had a revival fourteen winters in succession. I did not know how to account for it until I saw one of his members get up in a prayer meeting and make a confession. 'Brothers,' he said, 'I have been in the habit of praying every Saturday night until after midnight for the Holy Spirit to come among us. And now, (and he began to weep), I confess that I have neglected it for two or three weeks.' The secret was out. That minister had a praying church.

And so we could go on with many examples to show the place of prayer in revival and to demonstrate that every mighty movement of the Spirit of God had its source in the prayer rooms. The lesson of it all is that as workers together with God, we must see ourselves as responsible for the conditions which occur around us today.

Are we concerned about the coldness of the church? Do we grieve over the lack of people born again? Does our heart go out to God in midnight cries for the outpouring of His Spirit?

If not, part of the blame lies at our door. If we do our part, God will do His. Around us is a world lost in sin, above us is a God willing and able to save; it is ours to build the bridge that links heaven and earth, and prayer is the mighty instrument that does the work. And so the old cry comes to us, "Pray."

All revivals are dependent on God, but in revivals, as in other things, He invites and requires the assistance of people. The full result is obtained when there is cooperation between God and humans. To use a familiar phrase, "God alone can save the world, but God cannot save the world alone." God and us unite for the task, the response of God in proportion to our desire and effort.

Today, there is no shortage of preachers delivering great sermons on the need and nature of revival with elaborate plans for the spread of the kingdom of God, but praying preachers are very scarce. The greatest advantage we can have is someone who will bring the preachers, the church, and the people back to real praying. The reformer we need now is the praying reformer—to call the ministry back to its knees.

Daily Reflection

Revival has become an easy-to-use term for outreaches, an expected outcome of hard Christian work, or something that happened hundreds of years ago. But revival is as much a part of our lives today as it is connected with our prayers. Praying for a renewal of hearts, an outpouring of the Spirit, and a fresh understanding of Jesus's salvation should be integral in our own times of communication with God.

1. What is your understanding of a revival?
2. Do you ever pray for it? Why?
3. Do you agree with the statement, "We must see ourselves as responsible for the conditions which occur around us today"?
4. Do you have a heart for revival, to pray for it? Do you think God can give you one if you ask Him?

16

ARE SHORT PRAYERS ENOUGH?

"And he came to the disciples and found them sleeping. And he said to Peter, 'So, could you not watch with me one hour?'"
Matthew 26:40

While public prayers should be short and condensed, there is room and value in quick, instant prayer; in our personal conversations with God, time is essential to its value.

Much time spent with God is the secret to all successful praying. Prayer that is felt as a mighty force is the immediate product of much time spent with God. Our short prayers owe their efficiency to the long ones that came before them. The short, successful prayer cannot be prayed by one who has not persisted with God in a long struggle. Jacob's victory of faith could not have been gained without that all-night wrestling.

God's acquaintance is not made quickly. He does not give out His gifts to the casual or rushed visitor. To be alone with God a lot is the secret to knowing Him and of influence with Him. He bends to the persistence of a faith that knows Him. He gives His richest gifts to those who declare their desire for and appreciation of those gifts in constant, sincere persistence.

Jesus is our example, spending many nights in prayer. His custom was to pray a lot. He had His habitual place to pray. Many long seasons of praying make up His history and character. Paul prayed day and night. It took time from very important interests for Daniel to pray three times a day. There is no doubt that David's morning, noon, and night praying was very long. While we have no specific account of the time these biblical saints spent in prayer, the indications are that they consumed much time in prayer, and on some occasions, their custom was long seasons of praying.

The value of their prayers is not to be measured by the clock, but our purpose is to emphasize in our minds the necessity of being alone a lot with God; and that if this feature has not been produced by our faith, then our faith is weak and superficial.

The men who have shown Christ in their character, and have most powerfully affected the world for Him, have been men who spent so much time with God that it is a notable feature of their lives.

- Charles Simeon devoted the hours in the morning to God.
- Mr. Wesley spent two hours daily in prayer. "He thought prayer to be more his business than anything else."
- John Fletcher sometimes would pray all night; always, frequently, and with great earnestness. His whole life was a life of prayer.
- Luther said: "If I fail to spend two hours in prayer each morning, the devil gets the victory through the day."

Spiritual work is not easy work, and people do not always enjoy it. Praying, true praying, costs a serious amount of attention and time for which our bodies and minds are not keen. Very few people will make a huge effort when superficial work can be enough for the job. We can become used to our rushed, weak, quick praying until it starts to look good to us; at least it keeps up a decent appearance and keeps our conscience quiet—the deadliest sedative! We can ignore our praying and not realize the danger until the foundations are gone. Rushed devotions make weak faith, poor convictions, and questionable holiness. To be little with God is to be little for God. To cut short our praying makes our whole Christian character short, selfish, and messy.

It takes good, sufficient time for the full flow of God into the spirit. Short devotions cut the pipe of God's full flow. It takes time in secret places to get the full revelation of God. Little time and rushing only distort the picture.

Henry Martyn said about his own life that "the lack of private devotional reading and shortness of prayer through incessant sermon-making had produced much strangeness between God and his soul." More quiet time and earlier hours was his remedy.

Daily Reflection

In our busy lives, we often do not have the time for long prayers. We squeeze in what we can but often use the time commuting to and from work as our quiet time. Small, under-the-breath prayers become our common form of communicating with God, and we often feel as though this is sufficient. But from this reading, it is clear that it is not.

1. What is meant by "time is essential to its value"? What does this mean for prayer?
2. Do you find it easy to pray for a good length of time? Why?
3. What is the purpose of praying long, if we have already read that "the value of prayer does not lie in the number of prayers or the length of prayers"?
4. How would you rate your own prayer time with God?

17

PRAYER IS AN INHERITANCE

"Posterity shall serve him; it shall be told of the Lord to the coming generation; they shall come and proclaim his righteousness to a people yet unborn, that he has done it"
Psalm 22:30-31

The more praying there is in the world, the better the world will be; the forces against evil everywhere will be stronger. Prayer is a disinfectant and a preventive. It cleans the air and destroys the contamination of evil. Prayer is no fitful, short-lived thing.

It is not a voice that no one hears or is lost in the silence. It is a voice that goes into God's ear, and it lives as long as God hears holy requests—His heart is alive to holy things.

God shapes the world by prayer. Prayers cannot die. The mouths that said them might not be able to speak anymore, the heart that felt them might not beat any longer, but the prayers live before God. His heart is set on them, and prayers outlive the lives of those who said them; they outlive a generation, an age, a world. The people who have prayed the most and who have said the best prayers are immortal. They are God's heroes, saints, servants, and deputies.

A person can pray better because of the prayers of the past; a person can live holier because of the prayers of the past. The person who has said many acceptable prayers has done a great service for the next generation. The prayers of Christians strengthen the next generation against the devastating waves of sin and evil.

It is a terrible thing for a generation to find their censers empty of the rich incense of prayer. Their predecessors were too busy or too unbelieving to pray, and now the heritage left to them is only terrible dangers and sad consequences. But those whose fathers and mothers have left them a wealthy inheritance of prayer are blessed.

The prayers of Christians are the heavenly capital that Jesus uses to continue His work on earth. The great struggles and birth pains on earth are the results of these prayers. Earth is changed, revolutionized, angels move more powerfully, and God's policy is shaped as the prayers increase and become more effective.

It is true that the greatest successes in God's cause are created and carried on by prayer. God's day of power—the angelic activity and power—are when the church takes hold of its inheritance of faith and prayer. God's conquering days are when Christians pray. When God's house on earth is a house of prayer, then His house in heaven is busy with power in its plans and movements—His people are clothed with victory and His enemies are defeated on every side.

There can be no substitute, no rival for prayer; it stands alone as the great spiritual force, and this force must be present in our lives and active. It cannot be left out and ignored during one generation, nor postponed for any great movement to advance—it must be continuous and specific, always, everywhere, and in everything. Many people believe in the effectiveness of prayer, but not many pray. Prayer is the easiest and hardest of all things; the simplest and the most awesome; the weakest and the most powerful; its results lie outside of our human possibilities—they are only limited by God's omnipotence.

People must pray—pray for the advance of God's cause. Prayer puts God in full force in the world. To a person who prays, God is powerfully present; to a church that prays, God is glorious in power.

These days we are in desperate need of a generation of praying people, a group of men and women through whom God can bring His greatest movements more fully into the world. The Lord is not constricted within Himself, but He is constricted in us, because of our little faith and weak praying. We need a breed of Christians who will tirelessly seek after God—who will not let Him rest until He hears their cry. There is a demand for praying people who are thirsty for God's glory, who are open and unselfish in their desires, desperate for God, who seek Him late and early, and who will take no rest until the whole earth is filled with His glory.

Daily Reflection

This is an interesting view on prayer, likening it to economical capital in the spirit. It changes our thinking when we can begin to see that investment and reward are not always immediate, but transcends generations. In other words, our prayers today can affect our children, and their children tomorrow.

1. Do you agree that "God shapes the world by prayer"?
2. Proverbs 13:22 says, *"A good man leaves an inheritance to his children's children."* In terms of prayer, how does the meaning of this verse change?
3. Do you agree with the statement, "Many people believe in the effectiveness of prayer, but not many pray"? Why?
4. Do you believe in the effectiveness of prayer?

18

PRAYING IS OF THE HEART

"My son, give me your heart, and let your eyes observe my ways"
Proverbs 23:26

The heart is the savior of the world. Heads do not save. Genius, brains, brilliancy, strength, and natural gifts do not save. The gospel flows through hearts. All the mightiest forces are heart forces. All the most wonderful characteristics are of the heart. Great hearts make great characters; great hearts make divine characters. God is love. There is nothing greater than love, nothing greater than God. Hearts make heaven; heaven is love.

It is the heart and not the head that produces great preachers. The heart counts for a lot in Christianity. The heart must speak from the pulpit. The heart must hear in the congregation. In fact, we serve God with our hearts. Worship from the head does not mean very much in heaven. One of the serious and most common errors from the modern pulpit is having more thought than prayer, and having more head than heart in sermons. Big hearts make big preachers; good hearts make good preachers. A theological school that expands and grows the heart is the main purpose of the gospel. The pastor unites his people to him and leads them by his heart. They may admire his gifts, they may be proud of his ability, they may be moved and affected by his sermons; but the foundation of his power is his heart. His scepter is love. The throne of his power is his heart.

The good Shepherd gives His life for the sheep. Heads never make martyrs. It is the heart that surrenders its life to love and obedience. It takes great courage to be a faithful pastor, but only the heart can bring this courage. Gifts and genius may be brave, but it is the gifts and genius of the heart and not of the head.

It is easier to fill the head than it is to prepare the heart. It is easier to make a brain sermon than a heart sermon. It was the heart that brought the Son of God from heaven. It is the heart that will draw people to heaven. People of the heart are what the world needs to sympathize with its despair, kiss away its sorrows, have compassion for its misery, and alleviate its pain. Jesus was the man of sorrows because He was a man of heart.

"Give me your heart" is God's command to us. *"Give me your heart"* is our demand of others.

A professional ministry is a heartless ministry. When the salary plays a big part in the ministry, the heart only plays a little part. We can make preaching our business, and not put our hearts in the business. The person who puts self to the front in their preaching puts the heart to the back. The person who does not sow with their heart in his study will never reap a harvest for God. The prayer room is the heart's study. We will learn more about how to preach and what to preach there than we can learn in our libraries. *"Jesus wept"* (John 11:35) is the shortest and biggest verse in the Bible. It is the person who goes out weeping (not preaching great sermons), bearing precious seed, who will come back in again rejoicing, bringing the harvest with them.

Praying gives sense, brings wisdom, expands and strengthens the mind. The prayer room is a perfect teacher and classroom for the preacher. Thought is not only illuminated and made clearer in prayer—thought is born in prayer. We can learn more in one hour of praying than from many hours in the study. There are books in the prayer room that cannot be found and read anywhere else. We receive revelations in the prayer room that we cannot receive anywhere else.

Real heart-praying, praying by the power of the Spirit—direct, specific, passionate, simple praying—this is the kind of praying that belongs to the pulpit. This is the kind demanded of those who stand in the pulpit. There is no school in which to learn to pray in public but in the prayer room. Preachers who have learned to pray in the prayer room have mastered the secret of pulpit praying. It is a short step from secret praying to effective, live pulpit praying. Having no personal, private prayer results in cold, spiritless, formal praying in the pulpit. Study how to pray not by studying the methods and formats of prayer but by attending the school of prayer on your knees before God. This is where we learn to pray before God, and also how to pray in the presence of others.

Daily Reflection

This almost seems like an understatement, to say that prayer is of the heart. But, as people, we quickly turn to our minds and bodies to accomplish and understand everything, and so, it is necessary to remind us. The heart—soul or spirit—is what God is interested in. It is there that we connect, understand, and speak to Him.

1. What do you understand by the term 'heart'?
2. Why do you think God is more interested in the heart than the mind?
3. Read 1 Sam. 16:7. Why do you think we have such a different view on things from God?
4. How can we change this and see more of the 'heart'?

19

IS THERE SUCH A THING AS PRAYERLESS PRAYING?

"These people draw near to Me with their mouth, And honor Me with their lips, But their heart is far from Me"
Matthew 15:8 NKJV

Prayerless praying has no heart in its praying. The lack of heart deprives praying of its reality and makes it an empty and unsuitable vessel. Heart, soul, life must be in our praying; the heavens must feel the force of our crying and must be brought into sympathy for our bitter and needy state. A need that weighs us down, with no relief except in our crying to God, must be the voice of our praying.

Prayerless praying is insincere. It has no honesty at heart. We speak words that are not really what is in our hearts. Our prayers give formal words to the things that our hearts are not hungry for.

A prominent and godly preacher once abruptly and sharply rebuked a congregation that had just finished praying. He said, "What did you pray for? If God should take hold of you and shake you, and demand what you prayed for, you could not tell Him what the prayer was that has just died from your lips." Prayerless praying has no memory and no heart. A mere form, an assorted mass, a weak compound, a mixture thrown together for sound and to fill up space but with no heart or aim is prayerless praying. A dry routine, a dreary chore, a dull and heavy task is prayerless praying.

But prayerless praying is much worse than either task or chore, it divorces praying from living; it speaks its words against the world, but with heart and life runs into the world; it prays for humility but nurtures pride; prays for self-denial while indulging the flesh. Better not to pray at all than to pray prayerless prayers, for it is sinning, and the worst is to sin on our knees.

The prayer habit is a good habit, but praying by force of habit only is a very bad habit. This kind of praying is not after God's order, nor generated by God's power. It is not only a waste, a perversion, and a delusion, but it is a source of unbelief. Prayerless praying gets no results.

God is not reached, self is not helped. It is better not to pray at all than to get no results from praying—better for the one who prays, better for others. People hear of the wonderful results of prayer: the good promised in God's Word to prayer. But in their own lives, the huge difference between the results promised and the results realized causes them to doubt the truth. Christianity and God are dishonored, and doubt and unbelief are strengthened by lots of asking and no getting.

It is sad to neglect any attempt to pray, but there is an immense waste in the prayerless praying which is done—official praying, habitual praying. People love the form and shape of something after the heart and reality have gone out of it. We can find many examples of this in those who seem to pray. Formal praying has a strong hold and a strong following.

In contrast with this, what a mighty force prayerful praying is. Real prayer helps God and man. God's Kingdom is advanced by it, and good comes to man by it. Prayer can do anything that God can do. What a pity when we do not believe this as we should, and we do not put it to the test.

Hannah's defense against Eli's charge of hypocrisy was: *"I have been pouring out my soul before the Lord"* (1 Sam. 1:15). God's serious promise to the Jews was: *"Then you will call upon me and come and pray to me, and I will hear you. You will seek me and find me, when you seek me with all your heart"* (Jer. 29:12-13).

Let our praying be measured by these standards, "Pouring out the soul before God" and "Seeking with all the heart," and see how much of it will be mere form, waste, and worthless.

No more dry forms with dead, cold habits of prayer! No more sterile routine, with senseless performances in prayer! Let us get serious about doing the main task of men: prayer.

Let us work at it skillfully, to be adept in praying, to be craftsmen in this high art of praying. Let us be in the habit of prayer, devoted to prayer, filled with its rich spices, passionate in its holy flame, that Heaven and earth will be perfumed by its aroma, and nations will be blessed by our prayers. Heaven will be fuller and brighter, the earth will be better prepared for its bridal day, and hell will be robbed of many of its victims because we have lived to pray.

Daily Reflection

Prayerless praying is enough of a problem that Bounds addresses it. It seems like a contradiction, and it is—praying without really praying! He equates it to hypocrisy, to fulfilling a duty without any true conviction. We may not be able to easily identify with others, but an honest look at our own lives will reveal whether it is there or not.

1. Have you ever prayed for the sake of it—a duty? Why? How did you feel about the prayer?
2. Why is this a "source of unbelief"?
3. Why do you think we often fall into the trap of praying without really praying?
4. What is the solution to this kind of dead praying?

20

PRAYING WITH FAITH

"For by grace you have been saved through faith"
Ephesians 2:8

In studying the principles and procedure of prayer, first place must be given to faith. It is the initial quality in the heart of any person who wants to talk to the invisible God. They must stretch forth hands of faith and believe where they cannot prove. Prayer is simply faith claiming its natural yet marvelous privileges—its inheritance. True godliness is true, steady, and persevering in faith as it is in prayer. When faith stops praying, it stops living.

Faith does the impossible because it brings God to work for us, and nothing is impossible with God. How great is the power of faith! If there is no doubt in the heart, and no unbelief, what we ask of God will definitely come to pass.

Prayer projects faith on God, and God on the world. Only God can move mountains, but faith and prayer move God. When He cursed the fig tree, Jesus demonstrated His power. He then declared that mighty power was given to faith and prayer, not in order to kill but to make alive, not to curse but to bless.

When we look at the importance of prayer, we find faith standing right by its side. By faith, we are saved, and by faith, we stay saved. Prayer introduces us to a life of faith. Paul declared that the life he lived, he lived by faith in the Son of God, who loved him and gave Himself for him—that he walked by faith and not by sight.

Prayer is completely dependent on faith. It has no existence apart from it and accomplishes nothing without its companion. Faith makes prayer effective and must precede it.

"For whoever would draw near to God must believe that he exists and that he rewards those who seek him" (Heb. 11:6). Before prayer even starts, before its requests are made known, faith must have gone on ahead and asserted its belief in the existence of God. It must have agreed to the truth that God *"rewards those who seek him."*

This is the first step in praying. While faith does not bring the blessing, it puts prayer in a position to ask for it and helps us to believe that God is able and willing to bless.

Faith starts prayer to work—clears the way to the mercy seat. It gives assurance that there is a mercy seat and that the

High Priest waits for us and our prayers. Faith opens the way for prayer to approach God.

But it does more, it accompanies prayer every step it takes.

It is a steady companion, and when requests are made to God, it is faith that turns asking into receiving. And faith follows prayer, since the spiritual life into which a believer is led by prayer is a life of faith. The one main characteristic of the experience into which we are brought through prayer is not a life of works, but faith.

Faith makes prayer strong and gives it the patience to wait on God. Faith believes that God is a rewarder.

There is no clearer, more encouraging truth revealed in the Bible. Even the prayer room has its promised reward, *"And your Father who sees in secret will reward you"* (Matt 6:4).

But, faith does not believe that God will reward everybody, nor that He is a rewarder of all who pray, but that He is a rewarder of those who diligently seek Him. Faith rests everything on diligence in prayer and gives assurance and encouragement to diligent seekers after God, for they are the only ones who are richly rewarded when they pray.

We need to be reminded that faith is the one inseparable condition of successful praying. There are other considerations when we pray, but faith is the final, the one indispensable condition of true praying. As it is written: *"Without faith it is impossible to please him"* (Heb. 11:6).

Daily Reflection

Faith is an integral part of praying—believing what we are asking for. Without this piece of the puzzle, nothing can happen. It is important then to understand the relationship between these two if we are to lead effective Christian lives, praying and expecting God to answer and move.

1. What is your definition of faith?
2. Look at Hebrews 11:1. How does this relate to your definition?
3. Why do you think God puts such a massive condition on faith in the Christian life?
4. If "faith does not bring the blessing," what does it do?
5. How can we 'get' more faith?

21

PRAYER AND SUPPLICATION

"First of all, then, I urge that supplications, prayers, intercessions, and thanksgivings be made for all people, for kings and all who are in high positions, that we may lead a peaceful and quiet life, godly and dignified in every way. This is good, and it is pleasing in the sight of God our Savior"
1 Timothy 2:1-3

We have two kinds of prayer named in the New Testament: prayer and supplication. Prayer indicates prayer in general. Supplication is a more intense and special kind of prayer. These two—supplication and prayer—should be combined. Then we will have devotion in its widest and best form, and supplication with its most sincere and personal sense of need.

The word 'prayer' expresses the largest and most comprehensive approach to God. It shows the importance of this element of devotion. It is communion and intercourse with God. It is enjoyment of God. It is access to God. 'Supplication' is a more restricted and more intense form of prayer, accompanied by a sense of personal need, limited to the urgent seeking of something for a desperate need.

Pasquier Quesnel, the French theologian, said that "God is found in union and agreement. Nothing is more effective than this in prayer." Intercessions combine with prayers and supplications. The word does not mean prayer in relation to others. It means coming together, uniting with an intimate friend for free, unrestrained communion. It implies prayer—free, familiar, and bold.

Paul gives the various terms of prayer, supplication, and giving of thanks as the complement of true praying. The heart must be in all of these spiritual exercises. There must be no half-hearted praying, no diluting its nature, and no reducing its power if we want to be free from unnecessary anxiety that causes friction and distress, and if we want to receive that peace that passes all understanding. To pray, we must be sincere in our hearts, growing in spiritual character.

Prayer is sensitive and always affected by the character and conduct of the person who prays. Water cannot rise above its own level, and a spotless prayer cannot flow from a spotted, defiled heart. Straight praying is never born out of crooked conduct. The people behind their praying give character to their supplication. The fearful heart cannot do brave praying. Dirty, polluted people cannot make clean, pure supplication.

In Paul's Prayer Directory, found in Ephesians 6, we are taught to always be in prayer, as we are always in the battle. The Holy Spirit should be found by intense supplication, and our supplications must be charged by His life-giving and illuminating energy. We need to be alert to this intense praying and fighting. Perseverance is an essential element in successful praying, as in every other area of conflict. Christians are helped to victory by our prayers. Apostolic courage, ability, and success are gained by the prayers of the soldier saints everywhere.

In Paul's directions to Timothy about prayer (1 Tim. 2:8), we have a comprehensive verbal description of prayer in its different departments. They are all in the plural form: supplications, prayers, and intercessions. They declare the multifaceted, endless diversity and necessity of going beyond the formal simplicity of a single prayer and pressing forward to add prayer on prayer, supplication to supplication, intercession over and over again, until the combined force of prayers in their wonderful forms unite with combined power to our praying. The only measures of prayer are a limitless wonder and a limitless amount.

The one term of 'prayer' is the common and comprehensive one for the act, the duty, the spirit, and the service we call prayer. It is a condensed statement of worship. Prayer is the prominent, all-important essence, and the all-coloring ingredient of earthly worship, while praise is the prominent, comprehensive, all-coloring, all-inspiring element of heavenly worship.

We have a brief and comprehensive statement regarding Jesus' prayer habits in Hebrews 5:7: *"In the days of his flesh, Jesus offered up prayers and supplications, with loud cries and tears, to him who was able to save him from death, and he was heard because of his reverence."* In this description, we see the pouring out of great spiritual forces. He prayed with *"prayers and supplications."* It was no formal, tentative effort. He was intense, personal, and real. He begged for God's goodness. He was in great need and He cried with *"loud cries,"* made stronger by His tears. In agony, the Son of God wrestled. His praying was not playing a part. His soul was engaged, and all His energy and strength were strained. Let us pause and look at Him and learn how to pray sincerely and truly. Let us learn how to win in an agony of prayer that seems to be kept from us.

Our prayer must pass into strenuous, insistent, personal supplication, and thanksgiving must bloom into full flower. Our exposed condition of heart must be brought to the knowledge of God, by prayer and supplication, with thanksgiving. The peace of God will keep the heart and thoughts, fixed and fearless. Peace—deep, exhaustless, wide, flowing like a river—will come in.

Daily Reflection

We often think of supplication as just another word for prayer, but as we can see in this reading, it is used to signify a specific type of prayer. In differentiating it from thanksgiving and normal prayer, it helps us to realize an aspect of prayer that is useful to us. When Paul encourages those in the Bible to offer up prayer and supplication, it becomes real and personal for us, too.

1. What is the difference between prayer and supplication?
2. Do you think it's necessary to have loud cries and be in agony to pray as Jesus did?
3. What has the character and conduct of the person got to do with supplication?
4. Thanksgiving is often mentioned as well; why do you think it often goes with prayer and supplication?

22

DO YOU TRUST GOD IN PRAYER?

"And those who know your name put their trust in you, for you, O Lord, have not forsaken those who seek you"
Psalm 9:10

Trust, in a record or historical fact, can be a very passive thing, but trust in a person energizes the quality, fertilizes it, and informs it with love. The trust which informs prayer centers on a Person.

Trust goes even further than this. The trust that inspires our prayer must not only trust in the Person of God, and Christ, but in their ability and willingness to grant the thing prayed for. It is not only, *"Trust in the Lord forever,"* but, also, *"for the Lord God is an everlasting rock"* (Isaiah 26:4).

The trust that Jesus taught as a condition of effective prayer is not of the head but the heart. It is trust that has *"no doubting"* (James 1:6). Such trust has God's assurance that it will be honored with large, satisfying answers. The strong promise of Jesus brings faith down to our present moment and counts on a present answer.

Do we believe without a doubt? When we pray, do we believe, not that we will receive the things we ask for in the future, but that we receive them, then and there? How we need to pray; *"Increase our faith"* (Luke 17:5) until the doubt is gone, and complete trust claims the promised blessings as its own.

This is not easy. It is only reached after many failures, much praying, lots of waiting, and many trials of faith. May our faith increase until we realize and receive all the fullness there is in that Name which guarantees to do so much.

Our Lord puts trust as the very foundation of praying. The background of prayer is trust. The whole of Christ's ministry and work depended on complete trust in His Father. The center of trust is God. Mountains of difficulties and all other obstacles to prayer are moved out of the way by trust and faith. When trust is perfect and without doubt, prayer is simply the hand stretched out, ready to receive. Trust perfected is prayer perfected. Trust looks to receive what was asked for and gets it. Trust is not a belief that God can bless, that He will bless, but that He does bless, here and now. Trust always operates in the present tense. Hope looks toward the future. Trust looks to the present. Hope expects.

Trust possesses. Trust receives what prayer acquires. So what prayer always needs is abundant trust.

The lack of trust and the failure of the disciples to do what they were sent out to do is seen in the case of the lunatic son, who was brought by his father to them. They attempted to cast out the demon from the boy but failed. The demon was too much for them, they were humiliated, and then Jesus comes with a rebuke.

What was their problem? They had been lazy in growing their faith by prayer and, as a consequence, their trust failed. They did not trust God, Jesus, His mission, or their own. It is the same in the church. Failure has resulted from a lack of trust or a weakness of faith—from a lack of prayer. Many failures in revival efforts can be traced to the same cause. Faith was not nurtured and made powerful by prayer. Neglecting a quiet time results in most spiritual failure. Being on our knees in personal communion with God is the only way that we will have Him with us in our personal struggles or in our efforts to convert sinners.

Jesus always put trust in Him, and the divinity of His mission, in the forefront. He gave no definition of trust, and He made no theological discussion of or analysis of it; He knew that men would see what faith was by what faith did. When faith was freely exercised, trust grew spontaneously in His presence. It was the product of His work, His power, and His Person. Trust is too simple for verbal definition; too joyful and spontaneous for theological terminology. The simplicity of trust is what confuses and amazes many people. They look around for some great thing to happen, while all the time *"'the word is near you, in your mouth and in your heart' (that is, the word of faith that we proclaim)"* (Rom. 10:8).

Daily Reflection

Prayer hinges on trust as much as it does on faith. Without trust, we cannot truly believe in the promises and the ability of the One we are asking. This would set the prayer against itself. But realizing who God is, that He will do what He says, and that He has our best interests at heart, changes the way we ask. There is no more doubt. This kind of prayer succeeds.

1. Why does trust in God go much deeper than trusting something or someone?
2. Look at Proverbs 3:5. Why do you think it was important for the writer to mention the difference between our whole 'heart' and our 'understanding' in relation to trust?
3. Do you find it easy or difficult to trust God? Why?
4. Why do you think trust in God can be confusing to other people?

23

PASSIONATE AND FERVENT PRAYER

"The effective, fervent prayer of a righteous man avails much"
James 5:16 NKJV

Prayer without passion stakes nothing on the issue, because it has nothing to stake. It comes with empty hands; hands that are lazy, as well as empty, which have never learned the lesson of clinging to the cross.

Prayer without passion has no heart in it; it is an empty thing, an unfit vessel. Heart, soul, and life must find their place in all real praying. Heaven must feel the force of this crying to God.

Paul was a good example of someone who possessed a fervent spirit of prayer. His requests were all-consuming, centered immovably on the object of his desire and the God who was able to meet it.

In Colossians 4:12, we have the same word as passion and fervency, but translated differently: *"Epaphras... always struggling on your behalf in his prayers."* Paul charged the Romans to *"strive together with me in your prayers"* (Rom. 15:30). He was asking them to help him in his struggle with prayer. The word means to enter into a contest, to fight against adversaries. It means to engage with passionate zeal to endeavor to obtain.

Prayers must be red hot. It is the fervent prayer that is effective and that succeeds. The coldness of the spirit blocks praying; prayer cannot live in a wintry atmosphere. Chilly surroundings freeze and dry up the springs of supplication. It takes fire to make prayers go. The warmth of the soul creates an atmosphere favorable to prayer because it is favorable to passion. By flame, prayer ascends to heaven. But the fire is not fuss, heat, or noise. Heat is intensity—something that glows and burns.

God wants warm-hearted servants. The Holy Spirit comes as a fire to live in us; we are to be baptized, with the Holy Spirit and with fire. Passion is the warmth of the soul. If Christianity does not set us on fire, it is because we have frozen hearts. God lives in a flame; the Holy Spirit comes down in fire. To be absorbed in God's will, to be so sincere about doing it that our whole being takes fire, is the qualifying condition of the person who would engage in effective prayer.

Many of the great Bible characters were examples of having passionate spirits when seeking God.

- "*My soul is consumed with longing for your rules at all times*" (Psalm 119:20).
- "*As a deer pants for flowing streams, so pants my soul for you, O God. My soul thirsts for God, for the living God. When shall I come and appear before God?*" (Psalm 42:1-2).
- "*O Lord, all my longing is before you; my sighing is not hidden from you*" (Psalm 38:9).

Passion is in the heart, not in the brain, nor the intellectual faculties of the mind. Passion, therefore, is not an expression of the intellect. The passion of spirit is something far above poetical fancy or sentimental imagery. It is not a preference, liking, or disliking of something. It is the beat and action of the emotional nature.

We cannot create passion of spirit when we want, but we can pray to God to put it in us. Then, it is ours to nourish and cherish, to guard and prevent its decline. The process of personal salvation is not only to pray, to express our desires to God, but to acquire a passionate spirit—to grow and look after it. It is never out of place to pray to God to beget within us and to keep alive the spirit of fervent prayer.

Passion has to do with God, just as prayer has to do with Him. Desire always has an objective. If we desire at all, we desire something. The degree of passion with which we shape our spiritual desires will always determine the sincerity of our praying. In relation to this, Adoniram Judson says:

A persevering spirit, a great burdened desire, belongs to prayer. A fervency strong enough to drive away sleep, which devotes and inflames the spirit, and which puts away all earthly concerns, all this belongs to wrestling, prevailing prayer. The Spirit, the power, the air, and food of prayer is in such a spirit.

Prayer must be clothed with passion, strength, and power. It is the force that, centered on God, determines the outlay of Himself for earthly good. Men who are passionate in spirit are determined to attain righteousness, truth, grace, and all other powerful virtues that are part of the character of a true child of God.

Daily Reflection

Passion is something we often associate with romantic or artistic ventures, but we are called to be passionate in our prayers. This is not an emotional response that comes from feelings that we cannot control, but a determined and focused desire to see more in the spirit, more of God. Passion and fervency come from a deep need to be in God's presence and see Him move in our lives.

1. What do you understand by "passion for Jesus"?
2. Why is it important for the "heart, soul, and life" to be part of passionate prayer?
3. If we cannot create passion of spirit, how do we get it?

4. Bounds mentions the Holy Spirit a few times here in relation to passionate prayer. What link do you think there is between the Spirit and passionate prayer?

24

OBEYING AND PRAYING

"And this is love, that we walk according to his commandments; this is the commandment, just as you have heard from the beginning, so that you should walk in it"
2 John 1:6

Obedience is a high virtue, a soldier quality. To obey belongs to the soldier. It is his first and last lesson, and he must learn how to practice it all the time, without question, without complaint. Obedience is faith in action and is the test of love.

"If you keep my commandments, you will abide in my love, just as I have kept my Father's commandments and abide in his love" (John 15:10).

What a marvelous statement of the relationship created and maintained by obedience! The Son of God is held in the arms of the Father's love, because of His obedience! And the factor which enables the Son of God to abide in His Father's love is revealed in His own statement, *"I always do the things that are pleasing to him"* (John 8:29).

The gift of the Holy Spirit depends on loving obedience:

"If you love me, you will keep my commandments. And I will ask the Father, and he will give you another Helper, to be with you forever" (John 14:15-16).

What is obedience? It is doing God's will: it is keeping His commandments. Obedience is love, fulfilling every command, love expressing itself. Obedience is not a hard demand made on us, any more than the service a husband does for his wife, or a wife for her husband. Love delights to obey, and pleases the one it loves. There are no hardships in love. There may be requirements, but no irritation or displeasure in fulfilling them. There are no impossible tasks for love.

With simplicity, John says, *"whatever we ask we receive from him, because we keep his commandments and do what pleases him"* (1 John 3:22).

This is obedience, running ahead of every command. It is love, obeying by anticipation. God's commands are not heavy. Their ways are pleasant, and their paths are full of peace. Obedience is not a hard one. *"For my yoke is easy, and my burden is light"* (Matt. 11:30).

Obedience can ask with boldness at the throne of grace, and those who exercise it are the only ones who can ask. The disobedient people are shy and embarrassed in their approach and hesitant in their supplication. They are blocked by their wrong-doing. The requesting, obedient child comes into the presence of his father with confidence and boldness. His consciousness of obedience gives him courage and frees him from the fear that comes from disobedience.

"The Christian's trade," says Luther, "is prayer." But as Christians, we have another trade to learn, before we go on to learn the secrets of the trade of prayer. We must learn the skill of perfect obedience to the Father's will. Obedience follows love, and prayer follows obedience. Observing God's commandments accompanies real praying.

Obedience to God helps faith as no other attribute possibly can. When we are obedient—recognizing the validity and supremacy of God's commands—faith is no longer a superhuman task. There is no more huge effort to do it. Obedience to God makes it easy to believe and trust God. Where the spirit of obedience takes over the heart; where the will is perfectly surrendered to God; where there is an established purpose to obey God, faith almost believes itself. Faith becomes almost involuntary. After obedience, it is, naturally, the next step, and it is easily taken. The difficulty in prayer is not with faith, but with obedience, which is faith's foundation.

We must observe our obedience, to the loyalty of our heart to God, if we want to pray well and desire to get the most out of our praying. Obedience is the groundwork of effective praying; this is what brings us near to God.

The lack of obedience in our lives breaks down our praying. Often, our life is in revolt, and this puts us in a place where praying is almost impossible unless it is to ask for forgiveness and mercy. Disobedient living produces poor praying. Disobedience closes the door of the inner courts and blocks the way to the Holy of holies. No one can pray—really pray— who does not obey.

The will must be surrendered to God as a condition for successful praying. Everything about us gets its coloring from our inner character. The secret will makes character and controls our conduct. The will, therefore, plays an important part in successful praying. There can be no rich and true praying if the will is not completely and fully surrendered to God. This loyalty to God is an essential condition of the best, truest, and most effective praying. We have "simply got to trust and obey; there's no other way, to be happy in Jesus, but to trust, and obey!"

Daily Reflection

Obedience is often misunderstood as simply doing something, but as we have seen, habitual, ritualistic praying is not obedience but dead works. Having a heart of obedience is the key—a heart that wants to follow after God. It is important, then, to have this kind of heart in order for our prayers to be those that are acceptable to God.

1. "Obedience is love." What do you understand by this statement?
2. How does obedience help faith?
3. What has our will got to do with obedience?
4. Read 1 Samuel 15:22. What does this mean in relation to prayer and obedience?

25

BY PRAYER AND THANKSGIVING

"Continue steadfastly in prayer, being watchful in it with thanksgiving"
Colossians 4:2

Prayer, praise, and thanksgiving all go together. A close relationship exists between them. Praise and thanksgiving are so alike that it is not easy to distinguish between them or define them separately. The Bible joins these three things together. The Psalms are filled with many songs of praise and hymns of thanksgiving, all pointing back to the results of prayer. Thanksgiving is the expression of gratitude to God for the mercies received. Gratitude is an involuntary emotion of the soul, while thanksgiving is the voluntary expression of gratitude.

Thanksgiving is just what the word means—giving thanks to God. It is giving something to God in words that we feel in our hearts for the blessings we have received. Gratitude comes from knowing the goodness of God. It comes from serious meditation on what God has done for us. Both gratitude and thanksgiving point to, and have to do with, God and His mercies. The heart is consciously grateful to God. The soul expresses its heartfelt gratitude to God in words or acts.

Gratitude comes from meditation on God's grace and mercy. *"The Lord has done great things for us; we are glad"* (Psalm 126:3). Praise comes from gratitude and a conscious obligation to God for mercies given. As we think of the mercies we have received, the heart is moved to gratitude.

Love is the child of gratitude. Love grows as gratitude is felt, and then breaks out into praise and thanksgiving to God: *"I love the Lord, because he has heard my voice and my pleas for mercy. Because he inclined his ear to me, therefore I will call on him as long as I live"* (Psalm 116:1-2). Answered prayers cause gratitude, and gratitude brings out love that will not stop praying.

Gratitude and thanksgiving always look back at the past and the present. But prayer always looks to the future. Thanksgiving deals with things already received. Prayer deals with things desired, asked for, and expected. Prayer turns to gratitude and praise when the things asked for have been given by God.

As prayer brings things to us that lead to gratitude and thanksgiving, praise and gratitude promote prayer and bring more praying and better praying.

Gratitude and thanksgiving are opposed to the complaints and grumbling at God's dealings with us. Gratitude and complaining are never in the same heart at the same time. An unappreciative spirit has no place with gratitude and praise. And true prayer corrects complaining and promotes gratitude and thanksgiving. Dissatisfaction and discontentment are enemies of gratitude and thanksgiving.

Paul wrote:

- *"And be thankful... admonishing one another in all wisdom, singing psalms and hymns and spiritual songs, with thankfulness in your hearts to God"* (Col. 3:15-16).
- *"Continue steadfastly in prayer, being watchful in it with thanksgiving"* (Col. 4:2).
- *"Rejoice always, pray without ceasing, give thanks in all circumstances; for this is the will of God in Christ Jesus for you"* (1 Thess. 5:16-18).
- *"In everything by prayer and supplication with thanksgiving let your requests be made known to God"* (Phi. 4:6).

Wherever there is true prayer, there thanksgiving and gratitude are close by. Thanksgiving follows answered prayer just as day succeeds night.

True prayer and gratitude lead to full consecration, and consecration leads to more praying and better praying. A consecrated life is both a prayer life and a thanksgiving life.

Giving thanks is the life of prayer. It is its fragrance and music, its poetry and its crown.

God does much for us in answer to prayer, but we need many gifts from Him, and for those, we must pray specifically. We are to be special and specific in supplication and thanksgiving, bringing our requests, the things we need, the things we greatly desire, to God. And with it all, accompanying all these requests, there must be thanksgiving.

It is a wonderful thought that what we are called to do on earth—to praise and give thanks—the angels in heaven and the saints are doing also. It is also wonderful to think of the glorious hope God wants us to do on earth, which we will be busy doing throughout eternity. Praise and thanksgiving will be our tasks when we are in heaven, and we will never grow tired of it.

Daily Reflection

Thanksgiving is one of the understated, and often the most forgotten, aspect of prayer. We spend most of our time asking God for many things, but we do not thank Him enough for all that He does. To God, it is equally important to hear our gratitude, as it places us in the right attitude of heart before Him. To practice giving thanks more will only strengthen our prayers.

1. What do prayer, praise, and thanksgiving have in common?
2. According to the reading, where does gratitude come from?
3. What does it mean that "true prayer and gratitude lead to full consecration"?

4. Read 1 Thess. 5:18. Why do you think thanking God is part of God's will for us in Jesus?

26

CAN PRAYER STILL BRING MIRACLES?

"The prayer of a righteous person has great power as it is working"
James 5:16

When we look at Jesus' miracles, many were performed unconditionally—without being asked to do so—to glorify God and to show His own glory and power. Many miracles were performed when He was moved by suffering and needs, but some were performed in answer to the prayers of those who were afflicted or prayers of the friends of those who were afflicted.

In these conditional miracles, faith is the priority and prayer is faith's agent. An example of the importance of faith as the condition on which the exercise of Christ's power was based, or the channel through which it flowed, is seen in a visit to Nazareth.

"And he could do no mighty work there, except that he laid his hands on a few sick people and healed them. And he marveled because of their unbelief" (Mark 6:5-6).

The people at Nazareth may have prayed for Jesus to raise their dead, open the eyes of the blind, or heal the lepers, but it was in vain. The lack of faith restrains the exercise of God's power, paralyzes the arm of Christ, and turns to death all signs of life. Unbelief is the one thing that seriously hinders God in doing mighty works. Prayer must always be based on and backed with faith.

The miracle of miracles, the raising of Lazarus from the dead, was remarkable by the prayer that went with it. It was not a prayer for help. It was one of thanksgiving and assured confidence.

"Father, I thank you that you have heard me. I knew that you always hear me, but I said this on account of the people standing around, that they may believe that you sent me" (John 11:41-42).

It was mainly a prayer for the benefit of those who were present, that they might know that God was with Him because He had answered His prayers, and that faith in God might be ignited in their hearts.

Answered prayers are sometimes the most convincing and faith-creating forces. Unanswered prayers chill the atmosphere and freeze the soil of faith. If Christians knew how to pray to have evident, immediate, and demonstrative answers from God, faith would be more widely spread, more common, more profound, and would be a much more powerful force in the world.

What a valuable lesson of faith and intercessory prayer the miracle of healing the centurion's servant is! The simplicity and strength of faith of this Roman officer are remarkable, for He believed that it was not necessary for Jesus to go to his house in order to have his request granted, *"Only say the word, and my servant will be healed"* (Matt. 8:8). This man's prayer was the expression of his strong faith, and such faith brought an immediate answer.

If we turn back to the Old Testament, we have many examples of prayer miracles. They knew the power of prayer to move God to do great things. Natural laws did not stand in the way of God when appealed to by His praying people. Miracles and prayer went hand in hand. They were companions—one was the cause, the other was the effect. The one brought the other into existence. The miracle was the proof that God heard and answered prayer. The miracle was the demonstration that God, who was in heaven, interfered in earth's affairs, intervened to help men, and worked supernaturally to accomplish His purposes in answer to prayer.

Prayer still works miracles among people and makes great things happen. It is as true now as when James wrote, *"The prayer of a righteous person has great power as it is working"* (James 5:16). Many events that are seen as logical will one day be seen to have happened because of the Lord's praying people.

Many do not understand this kind of praying because they have not learned it, and do not work at it. Many miracles should be worked by our praying. So why do we not see them happening? Is the arm of the Lord too short to be able to save? Is His ear closed so that He cannot hear? Has prayer lost its power because of too much sin and because love has grown cold? Has God changed from what He once was? We can answer 'No!' to all these questions. God can easily work miracles by praying today, just as He did in the old days. *"For I the Lord do not change"* (Mal. 3:6). *"Is anything too hard for the Lord?"* (Gen. 18:14).

Daily Reflection

Many people debate whether miracles still exist or if they were only for biblical times. But when God works, it is supernaturally by His power—that is a miracle, for it is something that is beyond our possibilities. God's work in our lives, in answer to prayer, is a miracle. When we realize this, we will see that we can expect Him to do great things in our lives if we believe.

1. What is the difference between unconditional and conditional miracles?
2. Why is faith important in miracles?
3. Have you ever seen God answer your prayers beyond what was logically possible?
4. Why do you think we do not see more miracles happening?

27

BE PERSISTENT IN PRAYER

"Praying at all times in the Spirit, with all prayer and supplication. To that end, keep alert with all perseverance, making supplication for all the saints"
Ephesians 6:18

Jesus puts persistence as a distinguishing characteristic of true praying. We must not only pray, but we must pray with urgency, intention, and repetition. We must not only pray, but we must pray again and again. We must not get tired of praying. We must be sincere, deeply concerned about the things for which we ask, for Jesus made it very plain that the secret of prayer and its success lies in its urgency. We must press our prayers on God.

He made it clear by sharing a simple, poignant parable about the persistent widow asking for help from a judge in Luke 18:1-8.

This woman's case was a hopeless one, but persistence brings hope from despair and creates success where there was none. There is no stronger case to show how tireless and determined begging succeeds where everything else fails. Jesus told them the parable to show that they should always *"pray and not lose heart."* He knew that people easily get tired of praying, so to encourage us, He gives this picture of amazing determination that conquers or removes all obstacles, overcomes every resisting force, and accomplishes its goals despite invincible barriers. We can do nothing without prayer. All things can be done by persistent prayer.

Another parable of Jesus enforces the same truth in Luke 11:5-13. A man goes to his friend at midnight for bread. His pleas are strong, based on friendship and the embarrassing demands of necessity, but all these fail. He gets no bread, but he stays and begs, waits, and succeeds. Sheer persistence succeeds where all other pleas and influences had failed.

The case of the Canaanite woman is a parable in action. She is told that Jesus will not see anyone. When she does gain access to Him, she is ignored. She does not give up and is rebuked by the stern and crushing statement that He is not sent for Her, that she is excluded from His mission. She is humiliated by being called a dog. Yet she accepts, overcomes, and wins with her humble, determined tenacity. Jesus' response is: *"O woman, great is your faith! Be it done for you as you desire"* (Matt. 15:28).

The first lessons of persistence are taught in the Sermon on the Mount: *"Ask, and it will be given to you; seek, and you will find; knock, and it will be opened to you. For everyone who asks receives, and the one who seeks finds, and to the one who knocks it will be opened"* (Matt. 7:7-8).

Without carrying on, the prayer may go unanswered. Persistence is made up of the ability to hold on, to press on, to wait without relaxing your grip, restless desire, and restful patience. Persistent prayer is not an incident but the main thing, not a performance but a passion, not a need but a necessity.

Prayer in its highest form and greatest success assumes the attitude of a wrestler with God. It is the contest, trial, and victory of faith; a victory not secured from an enemy but from Him who tries our faith that He may enlarge it—He tests our strength to make us stronger. Few things give such stimulated and permanent strength to the soul as a long, exhaustive season of determined prayer. It makes an experience, a new calendar for the spirit, a new life to our belief, a soldierly training.

The benefits and necessity of tenacity are taught by Old Testament saints. Praying people must be strong in hope, faith, and prayer. We must know how to wait and to press in, to wait on God and be sincere in our approaches to Him.

There is no encouragement or room in Christianity for weak desires, half-hearted efforts, lazy attitudes; all must be strenuous, urgent, and passionate. Strong desires and impassioned, unwearied insistence delight heaven. God wants His children unashamedly sincere and persistently bold in their efforts. Heaven is too busy to listen to half-hearted prayers.

If Jesus had not prayed with persistence, there would have been no transfiguration in His history, no mighty works in His career. His all-night praying filled His all-day work with compassion and power. The persistent praying of His life crowned His death with its triumph.

Too often we get faint-hearted and quit praying at the point where we should begin. We let go at the very point where we should hold on the strongest. Our prayers are weak because they are not fueled by an unfailing and resistless will.

God loves the persistent beggar and gives him answers that would never have been granted but for the persistence that refuses to let go until the request asked for is granted.

Daily Reflection

Persistence is required if we are to grow in prayer. It's the reason Jesus told more than one parable about it, to emphasize how important it is to our spiritual maturity. If we want our prayers to reach further than they do right now, then we will need to push in, persevere, and be persistent. It is not simply nagging, but holding on and believing.

1. Do you have tenacity in your prayers? Why?
2. Why do you think we often give up too easily before we receive what we are looking for?
3. Why is waiting such a difficult thing for humans?

4. Read James 1:2-4. What does this say about perseverance or steadfastness?

28

PRAYER: THE CURE FOR ANXIETY?

"Do not be anxious about anything, but in everything by prayer and supplication with thanksgiving let your requests be made known to God. And the peace of God, which surpasses all understanding, will guard your hearts and your minds in Christ Jesus"
Philippians 4:6-7

'Cares' are the epidemic evil of mankind. They are universal in their reach. They belong to man in his fallen, sinful condition. Our tendency toward unnecessary anxiety is the natural result of sin. Care comes in all shapes, at all times, and from all sources. It comes to every person of every age and class. There are the cares of the home, from which there is no escape except in prayer. There are the cares of business, poverty, and wealth. Ours is an anxious world, and ours is an anxious race. Paul's warning, *"Do not be anxious about anything,"* is very suitable.

The command is so that we might be able to live above anxiety and free from unnecessary care, *"In everything by prayer and supplication with thanksgiving let your requests be made known to God."* This is the cure for all anxious cares, for all worry, for all anguish.

Jesus warned and urged His disciples, *"Do not be anxious about tomorrow"* (Matt. 6:34). He was trying to show them the secret of a quiet mind, free from anxiety and unnecessary care about food and clothes. Tomorrow's evils were not to be considered. He was simply teaching the same lesson found in Psalm 37:3, *"Trust in the Lord, and do good; dwell in the land and befriend faithfulness."* In warning against the fears of tomorrow's prospective evils, and the material needs of the body, He was teaching the great lesson of complete, childlike confidence in God. *"Commit your way to the Lord; trust in him, and he will act"* (Psalm 37:5).

Paul's direction is very specific, *"Do not be anxious about anything."* Do not be anxious about any condition, chance, or happening. Do not be worried about anything that creates anxiety. Have a mind free from all anxieties, cares, and all worries. Cares divide, distract, confuse, and destroy unity, forces, and quietness of mind. Cares are fatal to weak holiness and are debilitating to strong holiness. How necessary it is to guard against them and learn the one secret of their cure—prayer!

What unlimited possibilities prayer has to solve the situation of the mind that Paul is speaking about! Only prayer can quiet every distraction, hush every anxiety, and lift every care from care-enslaved lives and care-bewildered hearts. Prayer is the perfect cure for every problem that belongs to anxieties, concerns, and worries. Only prayer can drive anxiety away, relieve unnecessary heart burdens, and save us from the sin of worrying over things that we cannot help. Only prayer can bring into the heart and mind the *"peace of God, which surpasses all understanding,"* and keep the mind and heart at ease, free from crippling concerns.

Paul says to the Corinthians, *"I want you to be free from anxieties"* (1 Cor. 7:32), and this is the will of God. Prayer has the ability to do this. Peter talks about *"casting all your anxieties on him, because he cares for you"* (1 Peter 5:7), while the Psalmist says, *"Fret not yourself; it tends only to evil"* (Psalms 37:8). What a blessing to have a heart free from all worries, exempt from unnecessary anxiety, in the enjoyment of the peace of God which passes all understanding!

Just before Paul's command to *"not be anxious about anything,"* he adds this encouragement:

"Rejoice in the Lord always; again I will say, rejoice. Let your reasonableness be known to everyone. The Lord is at hand" (Phil. 4:4-5).

This joyful, carefree, peaceful experience bringing the believer into joy, living simply by faith day by day, is the will of God. Writing to the Thessalonians, Paul tells them: *"Rejoice always; pray without ceasing, give thanks in all circumstances; for this is the will of God in Christ Jesus for you"* (1 Thess 5:16-18). Not only is it God's will that we should find complete deliverance from all worry and unnecessary anxiety, but He has ordained prayer as the method by which we can reach that happy state of heart.

Daily Reflection

Anxiety and worry are too common in our lives, especially as Christians. And yet, the Bible is very clear that we should not have to worry. According to this reading, it is because we do not pray often enough. Prayer is the key to curing all of our anxieties. If we learn to bring everything before God and trust Him, there will be no need to fret.

1. Do you worry about your life, the future, your family? Why?
2. Do you find it easy to 'cast' all your cares onto Jesus? Or do you mention them but keep holding onto them?
3. Read John 14:27. What do you understand by these words? Read the verses before and after—do they add any context?
4. How do you think prayer relieves us of our worries?

29

THE POWER OF INTERCESSORY PRAYER

"Brothers, pray for us"
1 Thessalonians 5:25

Paul prayed a lot and tried hard to motivate Christians about the importance of prayer. He felt the need for prayer so deeply that he tried to convince others of this invaluable duty. Intercessory prayer, or prayer for others, was a priority for him in prayer. It is no surprise, therefore, when we find him throwing himself on the prayers of the churches to whom he wrote.

By their devotion to Jesus, their interest in the advance of God's kingdom on earth, the passion for their relationship with Jesus, he tells them to pray, to pray unceasingly, to pray at all times, to pray in all things, and to make praying a business of praying. And then realizing his own dependence on prayer for his heavy responsibilities and hardships, he urges them to pray especially for him.

Paul needed prayer. He needed the prayers of others, he admitted this by asking for their prayers. Becoming an apostle did not lift him above this need. He realized and acknowledged his dependence on prayer. He longed for and enjoyed the prayers of all good people. He was not ashamed to ask for prayers for himself nor to urge Christians everywhere to pray for him.

Praying for him was a powerful agent in facilitating his visit to them. Paul's frequent request was that they would *"pray for us"* (2 Thess 3:1). We should judge the value of something by how often it is asked for and the urgency of the request for it. If that is true, then with Paul, the prayers of Christians were among his greatest assets.

The sincerity can be heard in his requests. *"I appeal to you, brothers, by our Lord Jesus Christ and by the love of the Spirit, to strive together with me in your prayers to God on my behalf"* (Rom. 15:30).

Prayers from others were valuable because they helped him. Great helpers are people who pray. Nothing helps us as much as real prayers. They supply our needs and deliver us from hardships. Paul writes to the Corinthians that his faith had been tested, and he had been helped and strengthened by God's deliverance. *"You also must help us by prayer"* (2 Cor. 1:11). What marvelous things has God done for Christians through the prayers of others! We can help others more by praying than in any other way.

Paul had many powerful forces in his ministry. His remarkable conversion was a great force, a motivating power, and yet he did not secure results in the ministry by the force of his conversion. His call to become an apostle was evident, but he did not depend on that for results in his ministry. Paul's path was clearly marked out and his career was made more powerfully successful by prayer than by any other force.

Paul urges the Christians to pray for him that he may be delivered from unbelieving people. Prayer is a defense and protection against the plans of evil people. It can affect people because God can affect people. Not only did Paul have unbelieving enemies to contend with, but many Christians were against him. This was the case in Jerusalem, and so prayer, powerful prayer, needed to be used to remove the strong force of prejudice.

Prayer on the Christian's part for Paul must be used for his safety, and also that a prosperous journey and God's will might bring him quickly and safely to them, in order to bless and refresh them as a church.

He needs help, help that comes only through prayer. So he begs other Christians to pray for him and with him.

By prayer, enemies are swept out of the way. By prayer, prejudices are driven out of the hearts of people. Paul's way to Jerusalem would be cleared of difficulties, the success of his mission would be secured, and the will of God and the good of the Christians would be accomplished. All these results would be secured by praying. Wonderful and worldwide are the results that can be gained by praying. If those who succeeded Paul had prayed as he did, if all Christians had been one with apostolical men in prayer, how wonderful and godly would the history of God's church have been! How unparalleled would its success have been! The glory of its millennium would have brightened and blessed the world many years ago.

Daily Reflection

Intercession is an important part of prayer, as it takes the focus off of ourselves, and what we need and want, and places it on others. It gives us an opportunity to develop spiritual compassion for them. It unites us in the spirit as we stand for other people and trust God to come through for them in their time of need. Our hearts become less selfish the more we are on our knees for others.

1. Do you find it easy to ask others to pray for you when you are in need? Or do you feel ashamed to do so?
2. Do you find it easy to pray for others? Why?
3. Why do you think God honors our prayers for others so much?
4. Have you ever experienced God answering someone else's prayer for your life or your prayer for someone else's life?

30

THE POWER OF A PRAYING PASTOR

"But we will devote ourselves to prayer and to the ministry of the word"
Acts 6:4

The apostles knew the necessity and worth of prayer in their ministry. They knew that their calling as apostles did not excuse them from having to pray, but made it an even more urgent requirement. They did not want other work to steal away their time and prevent them from praying, so they appointed deacons to look after ministering to the poor, then they could *"devote ourselves to prayer and to the ministry of the word"* (Acts 6:4). Prayer is put first, surrendering themselves to praying, putting energy, urgency, perseverance, and time in it.

If our church leaders had been as particular and fervent in praying for their people as the apostles were, the sad, dark times of worldliness and heresy would not have eclipsed the glory and stopped the advance of the church. Apostolic praying makes apostolic saints and keeps apostolic times of purity and power in the church.

The preacher is to give himself over to prayer for his people; not that they might be saved, but that they might be powerfully saved. The apostles gave themselves to prayer so that the believers might be perfect; not that they should have a little desire for the things of God, but that they *"may be filled with all the fullness of God"* (Eph. 3:19). Paul did not rely solely on his apostolic preaching to do the job, but he said, *"for this reason I bow my knees before the Father"* (Eph. 3:14). Paul's praying carried those who were born again farther along than his preaching did. Epaphras did more by prayer for the Colossians than by his preaching. He was fervent always in prayer for them that they *"may stand mature and fully assured in all the will of God"* (Col. 4:12).

Preachers are God's leaders. They are responsible for the condition of the church. They shape its character and give tone and direction to its life.

Much depends on these leaders. The church is holy, and the treasure it holds is heavenly, but it has the stamp of humans. The treasure is in jars of clay, and it has all the signs of the vessel. The church is made by its leaders. It will be what its leaders are: spiritual if they are, secular if they are, mixed-up if its leaders are. Israel's kings gave character to Israel's holiness. A church hardly ever turns against or rises above the belief of its leaders. Strong spiritual leaders, men of holy power, are tokens of God's favor—disaster and weakness follow after feeble or worldly leaders. Israel fell low when they had children to rule over them. No happy state was predicted by the prophets when children oppressed Israel and women ruled over them. Times of spiritual leadership are times of great spiritual prosperity to the church.

Prayer is one of the main characteristics of strong spiritual leadership. People of powerful prayer are people of power. Their power with God is able to overcome many obstacles.

How can a person preach a message that does not come fresh from God in the prayer room? How can he preach without having his faith motivated, his vision cleared, and his heart encouraged by spending time with God? What a pity for those in the pulpit who are untouched by the prayer room. They will be dry and without anointing, and spiritual truths will never come with power from their mouths. As far as the real interests of Christianity are concerned, a pulpit without a prayer room will often be barren.

A preacher can preach in an official, entertaining, or educated way without prayer, but between this kind of preaching and sowing God's precious seed with holy hands and prayerful, weeping hearts, there is a wide gap.

A prayerless pastor is an undertaker of all God's truth and for the church. He may have the most costly casket and the most beautiful flowers, but it is a funeral, despite how charming and wonderful he looks. A prayerless Christian will never learn God's truth; a prayerless ministry will never be able to teach God's truth. Could it be possible that years of glory have been lost because of a prayerless church? Could the coming of our Lord have been delayed because of a prayerless church? Has Hell been allowed to expand and fill its caves from the dead service of a prayerless church?

The best, the greatest offering, is an offering of prayer. If the preachers will learn the lesson of prayer, and use the power of prayer, the church will shine. *"Pray without ceasing"* (1 Thess. 5:17) is the trumpet call to the preachers of our time. If they will get their verses, thoughts, words, and sermons in their prayer rooms, we will soon find a new heaven and a new earth. The old sin-stained and sin-eclipsed heaven and earth will pass away under the power of a praying ministry.

Daily Reflection

This seems like it should be expected—a pastor that prays. And yet, they are people, just like us, and have similar struggles when it comes to prayer, just like us. It very quickly shows us that prayer is a great leveler for all of us; not even Paul or Jesus was above having to pray. The importance of talking to God remains for every one of us if we are to grow.

1. Do you agree that prayer does more than preaching?
2. What are the consequences of a church that does not pray?
3. Do you know any strong spiritual leaders? What are their prayer lives like?
4. What is your church prayer like?

31

WHATEVER YOU ASK IN MY NAME

"Whatever you ask in my name, this I will do, that the Father may be glorified in the Son"
John 14:13

Jesus taught us to come to the Father in His name. That is our passport. It is in His name that we are to make our requests known.

Truly, truly, I say to you, whoever believes in me will also do the works that I do; and greater works than these will he do, because I am going to the Father. Whatever you ask in my name, this I will do, that the Father may be glorified in the Son. If you ask me anything in my name, I will do it. (John 14:12-14)

How wide and comprehensive is that 'whatever.' There is no limit to the power of that name. *"Whatever you ask."* That is

His declaration, and it opens up a world of infinite resources and possibilities to every praying child.

The possibilities of prayer reach all things. Whatever concerns our highest welfare, and whatever has to do with God's plans and purposes concerning people on earth, is a subject for prayer. Everything that concerns us or the children of men and God is in *"whatever you ask."* And whatever is left out of *'whatever'* is left out of prayer. Where do we draw the lines on what is left out or limited by the word *'whatever'*? Define it, and search out and publish the things which the word does not include. If *'whatever'* does not include all things, then add to it the word *'anything.'*

Mark 11:24 says, *"Therefore I tell you, whatever you ask in prayer, believe that you have received it, and it will be yours."* Perfect faith always has what perfect prayer asks for. How large and unlimited is the action: *"whatever you ask."* How definite and specific the promise: *"it will be yours."*

This statement of Jesus about faith and prayer is very important. Faith must be definite, specific; an unlimited, unmistakable request for the things asked for. It should not be a vague, indefinite thing; it must be something more than an abstract belief in God's willingness and ability to do for us. It is to be definite, specific, asking for, and expecting the things for which we ask. *"And does not doubt in his heart, but believes that what he says will come to pass, it will be done for him"* (Mark 11:23).

Genuine, authentic faith must be definite and free of doubt. Not general in character; not just a belief in the being, goodness, and power of God, but faith that believes that *"what he says will come to pass."* As much as the faith is specific, so the answer will also be definite: *"it will be done for him."* Faith and prayer select the things, and God commits Himself to do those things that faith and persevering prayer choose and ask Him to accomplish.

As long as the faith and the asking are definite, then the answer will be, too. The giving should not be for something else that was not prayed for, but the actual things that were sought and named. *"What he says will come to pass."* It is all imperative—*"it will be done for him."* The granting is to be unlimited, both in quality and in quantity.

Faith and prayer select the subjects for request, thereby determining what God is to do. *"What he says will come to pass."* Jesus is ready to supply exactly, and fully, all the demands of faith and prayer. If the order to God is clear, specific, and definite, God will fill it, exactly in accordance with the terms given.

"You did not choose me, but I chose you and appointed you that you should go and bear fruit and that your fruit should abide, so that whatever you ask the Father in my name, he may give it to you" (John 15:16).

Jesus puts fruit-bearing and fruit-remaining, ripe and rich fruit, that prayer might come to its full possibilities in order that the Father might give. Again, we have the undefined and unlimited word *'whatever'* as covering the rights and the things for which we are to pray in the possibilities of prayer.

Nothing is too hard for the Lord to do. As Paul declared, *"Now to him who is able to do far more abundantly than all that we ask or think"* (Eph. 3:20). Prayer has to do with God, with His ability to do. The possibility of prayer is the measure of God's ability to do.

The *"all,"* the *"whatever,"* and the *"anything"* are all covered by the ability of God. The urgent appeal reads, *"Ask whatever you wish,"* (John 15:7) because God is able to do anything and all things that we desire and that He has promised. In God's ability to do, He goes far beyond our ability to ask. Human thoughts, human words, human imaginations, human desires, and human needs cannot in any way measure God's ability to do.

Daily Reflection

To see the word 'whatever' so clear and unmistakable like this challenges us. Bounds wants us to realize that it stretches as wide as the word is defined—whatever! When we begin to see the possibilities of asking anything in Jesus' name, our faith should grow wider as well.

1. What do you think of when you read "Whatever you ask in my name"?
2. Do you restrict yourself to asking God for things that you think He might be able to accomplish?
3. Why do you think that faith and asking need to be definite?
4. Do you believe God can do 'anything' and 'whatever you ask'?

ABOUT E. M. BOUNDS

Edward McKendree Bounds was born on August 15, 1835 in Missouri, the last of five children. After his father's death, he joined relatives in California during the gold rush but returned to Missouri to finish his education. He became the youngest practicing lawyer in his state at the age of 19 after completing his law studies.

However, his heart was set on joining the ministry, and after attending a revival meeting, he closed his office. He enrolled in the Centenary Seminary where he was ordained as a Methodist minister at the age of 24.

Despite being anti-slavery, he was called on to pledge an oath and post a war bond. His refusal to do both landed him in prison as a Confederate sympathizer. After a year and a half, he was released and filled the role of chaplain alongside the Confederate Army, where he was wounded and taken prisoner.

On his release, he swore loyalty to the United States and returned to war-torn Franklin as the pastor of a Methodist church there. His main method of bringing a spiritual reawakening to the region was to hold weekly prayer meetings—these sometimes lasted for many hours.

Following his approach to prayer, a revival broke out across the district. Soon, he was being called to preach and travel across the country, where he served in different churches. At the end of his pastorate, he became the editor of the St Louis *Christian Advocate*.

He wrote 11 books, 9 of them on the topic of prayer.

Bounds married in 1876 and then remarried in 1887 after his first wife passed away. Toward the later years of his life, he lived with his family in Washington reading, writing, and praying. His habit was to get up at 4 a.m. and spend time praying until 7 a.m.

He passed away on August 24, 1913.

REFERENCES

Crossway. (2001). *English Standard Version Bible*. Crossway Bibles.

Holman Bible Publishers. (2016). *The Holy Bible: NKJV New King James Version*. Holman Bible Publishers.

www.ingramcontent.com/pod-product-compliance
Lightning Source LLC
LaVergne TN
LVHW020425070526
838199LV00003B/276